Solutions for Early Childhood Directors

Dedication and Thanks

This book is dedicated to Actor John Michael, Princess Gracie, and Jackson, the clown, because they fill my life with unforgettable memories every day.

Thanks to all of my colleagues who shared their input and opinions during this process. A special thanks to my family and friends who shared the load so I could sit and write.

Kathy Charner, the miracle worker behind the scenes, you are a joy to work with.

Thank you, Dr. Jan Cooper Taylor at Mississippi State University, for teaching that Child Care Administration class so many years ago. See, I really did pay attention in class.

Thank you, Ken Rada Photography and Deb Walker, for the wonderful photographs.

Solutions

FOR EARLY CHILDHOOD DIRECTORS

Real Answers to Everyday Challenges

Kathy Lee

Photographs by Ken Rada Photography
Deb Walker
Illustrations by Kathy Dobbs

gryphon house
Beltsville, MD

Photographs: Ken Rada Photography and Deb Walker

Illustrations: Kathy Dobbs

Library of Congress Cataloging-in-Publication Data

Lee, Kathy H., 1968-
  Solutions for early childhood directors : real answers to everyday challenges / by Kathy H. Lee.
      p. cm.
Includes bibliographical references and index.
  ISBN: 978-0-87659-229-8
  1. Day care centers--United States--Administration. I. Title.
HQ778.63.L44 2003
372.71'2'068--dc21

                                        2003007092

Bulk purchase

Gryphon House books are available for special premium and sales promotions as well as for fund-raising use. Special editions or book excerpts also can be created to specification. For details, contact the Director of Marketing at the address above.

Disclaimer

The publisher and the author cannot be held responsible for injury, mishap, or damages incurred during the use of or because of the information in this book. Every effort has been made to locate copyright and permission information.

 Gryphon House is a member of the Green Press Initiative, a nonprofit program dedicated to supporting publishers in their efforts to reduce their use of fiber-sourced forests. This book is made of 30% post-consumer waste. For further information visit www.greenpressinitiative.org.

Table of Contents

Introduction

I will never forget my first job in administration. I was the assistant director of a non-profit, corporate child development center. I was hired about three weeks before the center was scheduled to open. Within my first three weeks as an administrator I sat in on about 20 employee interviews, worked with architects and builders, met with licensing reps, toured with about 50 prospective parents, and attended several important meetings with the corporate sponsor and the managing company for the child development center. There's more...I ordered supplies, arranged classrooms, created menus, organized employee and children's files, and watched a center open its doors for the very first time. There was no prior history, no prior administration—only the director, myself, and the staff we had hired. We were the first and only impression parents would have of this center at this point. We were setting the tone for future administrators and teachers. I was very fortunate to work under a super director. I learned by watching her interact with parents and staff, asking lots of questions, and shadowing her throughout the days. The managing company for this center was a terrific non-profit organization that believed in quality childcare. It put money into quality materials and quality staff. It encouraged us to set up the program according to NAEYC standards and, when we were eligible, apply for accreditation. It really was a dream come true for anyone wanting to work in management. I assumed all administrator jobs were the same as this one.

I have never been so wrong in my life. A for-profit company offered me a director's job, and I was confident that I was ready. After all, I had started one center from scratch! Ha! I took the job as director and envisioned my own version of the center I had just left. My new employer had hired me to be the director of a program that had not even broken ground. The building of this center was entirely different than the one from my previous experience. My confidence was soon shaken by high teacher-student ratios, angry parents, underpaid staff members, low morale, budget cuts, and burnout. I began to question why I worked in this field at all! What was I thinking?! I did not have a support system, I did not have books or magazines—I needed help!

Help soon came in the form of another employee of the company. She challenged me to use what I knew about child development and developmentally appropriate practices and try and make it work within the system. She suggested that I look at the center from the children's perspective: what is the day like for them? I began to ask myself what I could do to make it better within the reality of the situation. She also encouraged me to attend a director's training, which was one of the best things I ever did. I collected lots of good information, and I experienced real networking for the first time. I left that day with seven business cards of area directors that I could contact. And I did. When I moved away and left this company, I was thankful for the experience. I learned some hard lessons that helped me as I took on my next role.

When I moved to a new state, I had the opportunity to direct a church-affiliated child development center. Again, I was unprepared. With a church program comes a new set of issues, such as working with a board of directors and other church staff, the difficulties of sharing space, and a host of unanticipated situations. I was amazed at how different childcare could be, yet again. I found myself in a new state, in a new arena, without support. Again, help came from a nearby center director.

She invited me to a local church director's meeting. I met everyone I possibly could that day. I was so excited to hear about the similar issues other church administrators faced. Many of my questions were answered that day. A few weeks later, I attended the state NAEYC conference and gathered more helpful information. I soon found myself feeling comfortable in this setting. So, a couple of years later when the opportunity presented itself to direct one of the largest child development centers in my area, I jumped on it. I thought, one church center to another, this will be great!

During the next year I experienced more trials and character-building moments than I had in all the previous centers put together. I did wonder why the search committee kept asking me during the interview process if I thought I had a strong personality. I was curious about the focus they kept placing on staffing, but NOTHING prepared me for what I was about to face. After only two weeks as the new director, most of the staff signed a petition demanding my resignation and submitted it to the board. I was totally thrown! I had worked with a variety of staff members in the past—with master's degrees and with no degrees, with children and without children, with those who loved their job and with those who hated their job—but I had never seen this. I'll never forget sitting in the office of the minister of education weeping and thinking about resigning. However, I did not resign.

Parents were talking to each other, staff members were talking to parents, and staff members were talking to other staff, all stirring up emotions over the changes I was making. I was surprised because I tried to change only things that were absolutely necessary at first. But to them, it seemed as if I had turned the place upside down. I was fortunate enough to have a support system in place. I had subscriptions to many early childhood journals and magazines. I had attended many conferences, workshops, and training sessions for directors, and I relied on them all. I researched issues, talked with colleagues, and looked deep within myself for an answer. In the end, it took lots of dedication and hard work. It took patience and consistency. It took openness and honesty. It took time. When I resigned to pursue writing books and training early childhood professionals, I left what I believe was the best child development center in our city and I was proud of what we had accomplished. The staff worked together and cared about children, parents, and each other. The parents had a good understanding of child development, had realistic expectations of the teachers, and supported the center wholeheartedly. The board of directors functioned as a unit, supporting my work as a director and the entire program. The children, who were most important, were making memories and enjoying the experiences they were encouraged to explore on a daily basis. We had something special at that center, something I will never forget.

I do not regret any of the experiences and challenges I faced as a director. I know with each struggle came growth and knowledge. There were times I wanted to hang it up, but I am passionate about this field. We who have the honor to work with children and their families are so blessed. I consider my time as a director a true blessing.

When I decided to write this book, I had a vision for it, too. I wanted to provide administrators with something real, something honest. I was so fortunate to have people step in when I needed help most, but I know that is not always the case. There are times when we find ourselves searching for a solution and need it immediately. My hope is that this book will provide that for you. When you read this book, I challenge you to face each situation by staying focused on your vision for the children and adults involved in your program. I have included a "For More Information" section at the end of each issue. Take time to read some of the articles, call the people listed, and research the subject. I am sure you will find that process as helpful and informative as I did. Remember, you have the privilege of impacting many lives every day. Memories are being made the minute people step through the door. Enjoy your role as a director.

Challenges Related to Staff

CHAPTER 1

How to Advertise for and Recruit Staff

The Challenge

Most directors struggle to find great staff members. Due to the high turnover rate in the field of early childhood care and education, it seems as though we are always hiring. The question I hear most is, "Where can I find good teachers?"

Solutions

I suggest that you not rely on a basic newspaper ad that seldom yields the best results. Instead, try one of the following suggestions:

1. Call colleges in your local area that offer a child development/early childhood major and inquire if anyone would like to participate in an internship with your program.
2. Set up booths at job fairs at some of those same colleges.

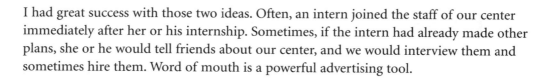

I had great success with those two ideas. Often, an intern joined the staff of our center immediately after her or his internship. Sometimes, if the intern had already made other plans, she or he would tell friends about our center, and we would interview them and sometimes hire them. Word of mouth is a powerful advertising tool.

Another way to find staff is to ask teachers if they know a colleague who might work well in a certain classroom. In one case, I called area directors and let them know my specific need. You never know when someone might apply for a job with another program that doesn't have an opening. (Okay, I know that's a long shot, but it has worked!) Sometimes parents in the program needed work, and we considered them, as well. Another idea is to advertise on early childhood websites. Ask your local or state association if they will allow you to advertise for a small fee.

Key Points to Remember

- Start with a newspaper ad (expecting little).
- Set up booths at college job fairs.
- Offer to host interns for local colleges' child development programs.
- Ask teachers and parents for suggestions.
- Network with other directors.
- Advertise on early childhood websites.

For More Information

* For complete bibliography, see pages 209-217.

- Find out which colleges and universities offer early childhood or child development programs in your area by using an Internet search engine.
- Check into advertising on a job website such as www.monster.com.
- Find the nearest AEYC affiliate group at www.naeyc.org.
- Read "Hiring the Right Person" by Annette Cannata Heng in the Sept/Oct 2001 issue of the *Child Care Information Exchange*.

How to Interview and Hire Staff

The Challenge

Finding the people to interview for positions is one thing, deciding which person to hire is another. Once, I interviewed a young woman with a bachelor's degree in child development. Right away, I knew that she was the person for the job, so I hired her on the spot. However, weeks later I was questioning my decision. The person I met in my office was not the same person who appeared in the classroom.

Solutions

I always thought I was a good judge of people, but boy did I mess up. I decided to re-think my interviewing and hiring process. I came up with a plan that had the following steps:

1. Interview the candidate on the phone.
2. Interview the candidate at the center with the director and mentor teacher (if possible).
3. Check the candidate's references (call their former administrators even if they are not listed as a reference).
4. Have the candidate meet the prospective co-teacher.
5. Ask the prospective employee to spend four hours observing in the classroom where he or she will be working.
6. Hire the candidate as a substitute teacher for two weeks.

I understand that this is a lengthy process for everyone involved. However, if you spend the extra time before you hire the employee, you are potentially saving many headaches later. At the end of this process, the prospective employee and I sat down for a "heart to heart" about the process that had just occurred. If either of us was not ready to make a decision, I always had the option of extending the substitution time or moving on to the next candidate. Once you are ready to offer your candidate a position, make a verbal offer and confirm it in writing. I never regretted the time or effort this process took.

When you begin to implement this plan, parents and staff may think, "What is she doing?" Stand firm. Explain to the parents that their child is so important that you would rather spend three to four weeks making sure this is the right person for their child's room than to spend three to four months trying to figure out how to get rid of a person who is not. Parents will understand; they want the best for their child too.

Co-teachers may be a little bit more impatient with this process. They must carry extra weight during this transition period. Remember to let them know that you recognize their extra effort and appreciate it. Treating them to a free lunch (or making them lunch), offering them an extra hour for their lunch break, or simply saying "thank you" more often shows them that you recognize their hard work and will do what you can to help them make it through this transition period.

Before you hire a candidate, take time to talk with the co-teacher who will be working with the person you hire. When possible, be sure both of you agree on your selection. You are the director and the final decision is yours, but that staff member will be spending the most time with the potential employee. If there is an initial problem with personalities or any other issue, you will have to address it.

Key Points to Remember

- Follow the six-step plan mentioned on the previous page.
- At the end of the two-week substitution, ask the current staff member for feedback about the candidate. Have a heart-to-heart discussion with the prospective employee. If either of you do not feel comfortable going forward, continue the substituting for a few more weeks.
- Get feedback from the co-teacher who will work most closely with the new hire.
- When you decide to hire someone, make a verbal offer, followed by a written confirmation.

For More Information

* For complete bibliography, see pages 209-217.

- Check out the website www.childcarebusiness.com.
- The book, *The Practical Guide to Quality Child Care* by Pam Schiller and Patricia Carter Dyke, is a super resource for this topic.

How to Conduct Staff Orientation

The Challenge

After I hired employees, I struggled to make time to properly orient them. New employees need more than the appropriate paperwork and the staff handbook. They must get to know the staff and the center.

Solutions

I implemented two new parts to our orientation plan. First, all of the staff worked together and made a video for the new employees. We started the video by welcoming the new employee to our center, even singing a greeting song for them. Next, several of the staff went over some of the basic policies for our center. For example, proper handwashing procedures, how to handle gossip, our teamwork mentality, and how space is shared were some of the topics presented to the new employee in a skit format. The staff really had a great time with this project. I know you can purchase great videos from many resources, but I thought this would make it more personal. New staff members enjoyed it, too. Ask your staff if this is something they might want to do, and if it is, plan to do it. Decide together what topics should be covered. Ask teachers to work in groups. Each group picks a topic they want to address. Give them ample time to create their skit. I encouraged the staff to use props and be creative. Not only was the video fun, informative, and original, the process of creating it was a great teambuilding experience. We asked a parent of a child in our center who worked in the film industry to videotape it for us, but this is unnecessary. Just grab a video camera and push "record." And have fun!

The second part of my new orientation plan was a scavenger hunt. During orientation, I gave the new staff member a list of "nitty gritty stuff" (see Sample List of Nitty Gritty Stuff on page 170 of the Appendix). For example, "Band-Aids can be found in every classroom in the 'booboo' box or in the office in the first aid kit." The new staff member was instructed to find everything on the list during the next week. She was allowed to ask her mentor teacher if she could not find something. At the end of the week, the staff member was given a scavenger hunt list (see Sample Scavenger Hunt on page 171 of the Appendix) consisting of the items on the "nitty gritty" list. The mentor teacher timed the new staff member to see how quickly she could complete the scavenger hunt. During the next staff meeting, we presented the new staff member with a "Congratulations!" sign and a piece of candy. If the staff member set a new record, we gave him or her a prize. The scavenger hunt was both informative and FUN!

Key Points to Remember

◆ Get together with staff and make an orientation video for new staff members. Include important policies and procedures in a skit format.
◆ Present the new staff member with a list of essential information ("nitty gritty stuff") and ask him or her to locate the items on the list over the next week.
◆ At the end of the week, give the new staff member the scavenger hunt list. The mentor teacher times the hunt.
◆ During the next staff meeting, congratulate the new staff member, and if he or she set a record for fastest time, present him or her with a small prize.

For More Information

* For complete bibliography, see pages 209-217.

◆ Read the article "Right From the Start: Changing Our Approach to Staff Orientation" by Margie Carter in the Sept/Oct 2001 issue of *Child Care Information Exchange*.

How to Use 15 Minutes Effectively

The Challenge

I remember my nervousness before I started my role as the "new director" at a center. I worried about the staff getting the wrong impression of me. I did not want to fall on my face. Even when I was a more seasoned director, I knew that I needed to maintain my connection with staff, although it felt as though I had little time to devote to the task.

Solutions

I decided to take **15 minutes** a day and write a personal note to each staff member. I shared my enthusiasm about meeting them and joining their team. I made it personal by mailing the note to each of their homes, not the center. If you've been the director of your program for some time already, use the note to communicate to staff that they are an essential part of your team and that you are happy they are working with you.

The day before I started my new job I took **15 minutes** and stopped by the new center (I called the current director and cleared everything first). I brought along some bagels for the staff. I strolled through the center expressing my enthusiasm about joining them and invited them to enjoy a bagel on their break. Continue to do this periodically, even when you are no longer the new kid on the block.

During my first week of employment I scheduled **15-minute** meetings with each and every staff member. The purpose of this meeting was simply to get to know the staff. I prepared for these meetings by:

◆ selecting an inviting environment—the staff lounge, outside on the playground, a picnic on the floor in the office
◆ providing drinks and snacks
◆ trying to find something I had in common with each staff member
◆ keeping it light—I invited each staff member to complete a questionnaire (see Sample Staff Questionnaire on page 172 of the Appendix) that related to his or her job. I gave them the option of writing down their answers or just verbally sharing them with me.

During my second week, I visited every classroom for **15 minutes**. I left my clipboard and pen in the office and just had a good time interacting with the teacher and the children. It is so important for teachers to see that the director is comfortable in the classroom. I used this time to begin to learn the names and personalities of some of the children, to help the teacher by offering her a bathroom break while I was there, and to get a feel for the classroom as a whole.

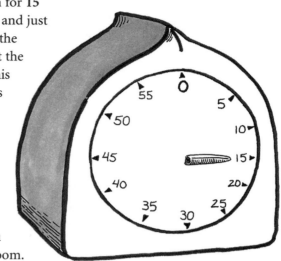

By my third week at work I had already invested in quality time with each staff member. You will discover that **15 minutes** does matter and that the entire staff will know that you are willing to invest time in them and their classroom.

Even after you are no longer the "new" director, continue to take 15 minutes a day to do something for your staff. By letting staff know that you care about them, you gain their respect, trust, and loyalty—three things every successful director needs!

Key Points to Remember

- Take **15 minutes** and write a note to each staff member, sharing your enthusiasm about joining the team or working with them. Send the notes to the staff members' homes.
- Take **15 minutes** to stop by the center before your first day. Bring a light snack, such as bagels or fruit.
- Take **15 minutes** with each staff member to get to know her or him.
- Take **15 minutes** and visit every classroom.
- Continue to make time every day to connect with staff, even after you are no longer the "new" director.

For More Information

* For complete bibliography, see pages 209-217.

- Read *Making the Most of Meetings* by Paula Jorde Bloom.

How to Train Staff

The Challenge

Each staff member comes to a center with her or his own ideas of early childhood and backgrounds that vary from no college degree and very little experience to a Master's degree and 20 years experience, or some combination thereof. Because of this wide range, I knew I had to figure out how to ensure that each teacher had a clear picture of our school philosophy and developmentally appropriate practices for young children.

Solutions

I decided to create a one-year training plan for each staff member (see Sample Professional Development Training Plan on page 173 of the Appendix). I did the following:

1. I sent out a survey (see Professional Development Survey on page 174 of the Appendix) asking all staff members to evaluate the areas where they felt they needed training and to formulate goals for their professional growth and development.
2. I met with each staff member to assess her or his survey and give my input. Together, we looked at conference brochures and targeted training sessions that would help the staff member accomplish the goals.
3. After the staff member attended a conference or training, I asked her or him to write down one change that she or he planned to implement as a result of the training. This was a good way to hold the staff accountable and encourage them to try some of the new ideas they learned.
4. After the first year, we included the training plan in the yearly staff evaluations.

Before you schedule a training session for your entire staff, it is important to interview the person who will be doing the training. One night, a highly recommended trainer came to our center to speak about discipline. I assumed that she understood child development, but I was horrified as I sat and listened to her guidance

techniques. Everything she said was reward and bribery based. I finally had to interrupt her and share my thoughts on the matter because I did not want my entire staff to hear this and think that this is what I expected in our program. If possible, before scheduling a training session, ask the trainer to send you information, such as a handout, so you know what will be discussed.

Key Points to Remember

◆ Send out staff surveys asking staff to evaluate their training needs.
◆ Meet with the staff individually to make a training plan.
◆ After the first year, develop training plans as part of your yearly staff evaluations.
◆ Before you schedule a training session, be sure you know what information the "expert" on the topic plans to present.

For More Information

* For complete bibliography, see pages 209-217.

◆ Read the following articles from *Child Care Information Exchange*:
   "Ongoing Growing—Overcoming Obstacles to Training Staff" by Connie Jo Smith
   "Ideas for Training Staff" by Margie Carter
   "Understanding Adults as Learners" by Nancy Alexander

How to Develop a Mentoring System

The Challenge

Have you ever had a discussion with a staff member that went something like this: "Kathy, I have worked here for years now and I am getting bored. I love the classroom, but I am ready for something else. I don't want to be a director, but I need new challenges." I have had similar conversations with many staff members over the years.

Solutions

After several conversations with staff members about a career ladder and a need for more challenges, I considered developing a mentoring system. I called other directors to see if anyone else had this type of system in their program and how it worked. I did find one director who had implemented this system, and she was very helpful. She told me that it was one of the best administrative decisions of her career. After I implemented mentoring in my center, I totally agreed. Mentoring provides many benefits for the staff, the center, and the director. The staff members who become mentor teachers have the opportunity to stretch themselves as professionals and share their experiences and expertise with other teachers. The center benefits by having additional staff members who receive extra training and who have the authority to step in when an administrator is absent. The director benefits because she or he has employees who see a career ladder in place, feel satisfied at work, and are supported in many areas.

How do you start a mentoring system? My suggestion is to start with one mentor teacher per age group. For my center we had four—an Infant Mentor Teacher, Toddler Mentor Teacher, Preschool Mentor Teacher, and School-Age Mentor Teacher. If you have a small program, two might be plenty. Create a job description for the position that includes the responsibilities that this new position requires in addition to being a classroom teacher. Some staff might think being a mentor teacher sounds great until they consider the extra work involved. Think about the qualifications needed to apply for this position and put it in writing (see Sample Mentor Job Qualifications on page 175 of the Appendix). Look at your budget and decide if a pay increase will be given for this position. If not, what will they get in exchange for their increased responsibilities? A bonus? A chance to go to a national conference? An extra week of vacation? I know these all involve money, but some more than others. Becoming a mentor teacher is considered a promotion. Part of what happens when you create a mentoring system is you create a career ladder in your center. You are offering a step between being a teacher and the director. With that step should come some type of monetary increase.

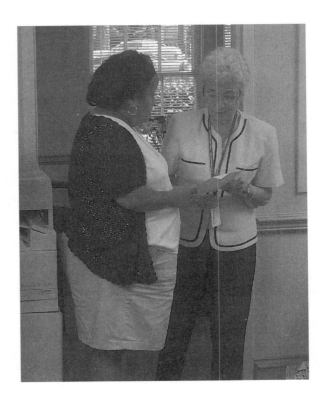

The next step is to advertise the positions to all of the staff currently on your team. Provide an application (see Sample Mentor Teacher Application on page 176 of the Appendix), job description, and qualifications to each staff member. Set a deadline for applications and schedule interviews with everyone who applies. Remember that these mentor teachers will be helping you train new staff, work with current staff, and, consequently, will be viewed as the leaders in your center. During the interview process consider these things: Does the applicant carry out the school's philosophy in his or her classroom? Does the applicant have a good working relationship with the staff and parents? Does the applicant show a desire to grow in the field? Be sure to ask everyone the same questions and be considerate of the feelings of applicants not promoted.

Once you have offered the positions to the qualified applicants and they have accepted the responsibility, meet with your new team. In this meeting thank them for their willingness to take on the additional responsibilities and encourage them to look at themselves as *fire starters** in their assigned area. Continue having team meetings with the mentor teachers once a month during a convenient time for the team. For me, it worked best to have these meetings during lunch a few days before our scheduled staff meeting. Team meetings help you stay in touch with what is going on with them and the group they are working with. The mentor teachers will also meet with their team once a month. For me, it worked best to include this time in staff meetings, but another time might work better for your center. During this time, mentors can go over specific issues with their group, plan any special activities for the next month, and discuss any problems they might be facing.
Fire starters are people whose enthusiasm and passion burn in them and create "fires" wherever they go with their flaming passions.

As I mentioned earlier, part of the mentor teacher's role is to assist in training new staff members. When considering an applicant, try to have the mentor teacher sit in on part of the interview. This gives the mentor teacher a chance to have input on who is joining his or her team. During the first week of employment, have the new staff member spend some time in the mentor teacher's classroom every day. The mentor teacher can model appropriate behavior and discuss important policies and procedures of the center. At the end of the week the mentor teacher can meet with the new staff member and discuss any issues that came up during the week. In addition, the mentor teacher can facilitate the scavenger hunt (see How to Conduct Staff Orientation, page 13). At any point, if the director or the mentor teacher senses that the new staff member needs additional help, the mentor teacher can initiate a conversation followed by additional training.

Implementing a mentoring system is something you will not regret. It promotes growth and teamwork. Some of the staff members who were mentor teachers with me are now directing their own centers. I remember a phone call from one former staff member who shared that she would have never had the guts to apply for an administrative position had she not been a mentor teacher first. She was more willing to take the risk because of the experience she gathered as a mentor teacher. Wow! I did not expect that as one of the benefits of implementing a mentoring system, but it was one of my proudest moments as a director. Don't be scared that some mentor teachers are going to leave your center; some will and some will not. The good news is other staff will probably be ready to jump in and try their hand at mentoring others. This is growth!

Key Points to Remember

◆ Decide if a mentoring system is for you.
◆ Check your budget to see if it can handle a pay increase or some other monetary compensation for the mentoring positions.
◆ Create an application, qualification requirements, and a job description for the mentor teachers.
◆ Open the application process to all staff who meet the requirements.
◆ Interview all applicants, asking the same questions to all.
◆ Choose applicants, being sensitive to those you do not promote.
◆ Meet with the new team of mentor teachers.
◆ Encourage mentor teachers to meet with their new team.
◆ Let the mentoring begin.

For More Information

* For complete bibliography, see pages 209-217.

◆ Read *The Power of Mentoring* by Wheelock College.
◆ Read "So you had a good day?" Educators Learn via E-mail" by Shelly J. Hudson in Spring 2000 issue of *Dimensions of Early Childhood*.

What to Do When Staff Are Promoted From Peer to Boss

The Challenge

This is a challenge in any industry in which a peer is promoted into a position of power and leadership. I had this situation happen in my center, when an infant teacher was promoted to assistant director. She went from hanging out as a peer in the staff lounge to hearing, "There's the boss!" when she walked by.

Solutions

First of all, I strongly believe in promoting from within whenever possible. It creates a sense of possibility and hope for those teachers who desire to grow and move into a management position. However, I understand why some centers choose to hire management-level positions from outside the center. It is not always easy to help a teacher transition to supervisor. Some of you might be experiencing this right now—two weeks ago you were a preschool teacher and chair of the resource lounge committee, but today you are the assistant director or even director.

For example, when I promoted Susan to assistant director, I did the usual—sent out a letter saying that she was now part of our administrative team and that I was excited that she would be serving in this capacity. In addition, I had a meeting with some of her closest co-workers to share my desire for them to show her respect now that she was their "boss." Susan did have a strong rapport with the staff and most of the staff's respect because they had worked with her and knew she practiced what she would now be preaching. In some ways, I saw her classroom experience with this staff as an advantage.

The main issues came with her "friends." I watched them try to ask Susan for favors instead of me. I watched them feel comfortable sharing a little more information than was needed about a parent or other staff. During Susan's training we discussed that this might be an issue. I suggested she simply follow the policies and procedures and she would be fine. She did a great job. Time helped with most situations. The longer Susan worked in the office, the fewer "friends" stopped in. She still went to lunch on occasion with some of the teachers and that was not a problem. In the beginning, when I needed to discuss an important situation or handle a disciplinary action with a staff member, I had Susan sit in on the meeting. I gave her specific assignments for the meeting to help her learn and gain confidence as a supervisor.

I called Susan the day I wrote this and asked for her side of the story. I wanted to represent her feelings as the one who went from teacher to administrator. Susan told me that she definitely was worried at first. She thought the other staff would resent her and not respect her. Actually, for most of the staff, it was exactly the opposite. As it turned out, the staff saw her as an ally because they knew she had been in their shoes. For the few staff who did have difficulty with her promotion, she worked hard at building a working relationship with them. She would go into their rooms first when she had time to offer bathroom breaks or just check in. Susan agreed that it became easier and that she gained confidence with time.

For teachers who were promoted from teacher straight to director, don't lose hope. My best advice to you is to find a mentor director or join a director's network as soon as possible. How do you find such a network? Think of a center director who you respect and give him or her a call or send an e-mail. The person might be the director of the NAEYC-accredited center two blocks away, your former director, or a more official mentor director through a local early childhood organization. Ask your mentor for some guidance. If needed, ask him or her if you can sit in on a meeting with one of his or her staff members to help you learn. In addition to finding a mentor director, be honest with your staff. Let them know that you view yourself as their official team leader, not their "boss." Yes, there will be times you have to make tough decisions—all leaders do. However, you hope the majority of the time is spent working together. Most professionals will be happy to see you or other staff members succeed and will be supportive.

Key Points to Remember

◆ Inform others of the staff member's new role and responsibilities.

◆ Encourage the promoted staff member to handle new situations that might arise with former co-workers.

◆ Be patient; time helps.

◆ If you are the former co-worker who is now the "boss," find a director who is willing to be your mentor.

◆ Honesty is the best policy. Calm staff members by expressing your desire to work as a team, not *boss* them around.

For More Information

* For complete bibliography, see pages 209-217.

◆ Read *Who, Me Lead a Group?* by Jean Illsley Clark.

How to Communicate Effectively

The Challenge

Lack of communication or miscommunication can lead to disaster in a childcare setting. There have been too many times in my career that things have fallen apart due to lack of communication.

Solutions

Communicating often clears up misconceptions and misunderstandings. Many times when problems occur, they can be traced to poor communication or a complete lack of communication. As a new director, I was so scared of conflict that I would not allow staff members to bring issues up in staff meetings. I lacked the confidence to open up group communication regarding the center. Looking back, I realize that this really hurt my relationship with the staff. Communication is always better than silence. Silence builds and usually causes explosions. I realized I needed to change my attitude—communication can't be my enemy; it must be my friend.

After my attitude adjustment, I made several communication changes in the center. I bought several wipe-off boards and placed one next to the time clock, one outside my office door, and one in the staff lounge/resource room. The wipe-off board next to the time clock was my main source of general communication with the staff. Every morning I informed staff of absences and substitutes, reminded them of field trips or special guests, and ended with a poem or simple words of encouragement.

The wipe-off board outside of my office was for the staff to leave messages for me. I wanted to accomplish several things with this board so I bought a combination wipe-off/calendar/cork board. I used the calendar to inform staff of my whereabouts and plans for that month as well as center-related dates. The general wipe-off area was used for reminders from staff, for example, "We are out of glue." The cork area was used for private notes. If a staff member needed to talk to me and did not feel comfortable writing it for everyone to see they could write a note, place it in an envelope, and tack it on the board. This board was great! The third board in the staff lounge/resource room was for staff to write notes to each other. Some of the notes were just for fun. Some communicated pertinent information, for example, "I need 10 egg cartons for an activity next week. Would everyone bring in one egg carton?" All three boards met a communication need. If you cannot afford to buy all three at once, I suggest starting with the one next to the time clock. Add the others as your budget allows.

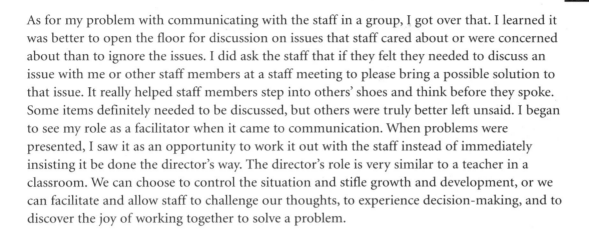

As for my problem with communicating with the staff in a group, I got over that. I learned it was better to open the floor for discussion on issues that staff cared about or were concerned about than to ignore the issues. I did ask the staff that if they felt they needed to discuss an issue with me or other staff members at a staff meeting to please bring a possible solution to that issue. It really helped staff members step into others' shoes and think before they spoke. Some items definitely needed to be discussed, but others were truly better left unsaid. I began to see my role as a facilitator when it came to communication. When problems were presented, I saw it as an opportunity to work it out with the staff instead of immediately insisting it be done the director's way. The director's role is very similar to a teacher in a classroom. We can choose to control the situation and stifle growth and development, or we can facilitate and allow staff to challenge our thoughts, to experience decision-making, and to discover the joy of working together to solve a problem.

Key Points to Remember

- Acknowledge that communication is your friend.
- Purchase several wipe-off boards for your center.
- Place one board outside of your office, one next to the time clock, and another in the staff lounge. Use them often!
- Think of yourself as a facilitator when it comes to communication. Allow others to express opinions and offer solutions when problems arise.

For More Information

* For complete bibliography, see pages 209-217.

- Read *Are You an Active Listener?* by Richard G. Ensman, Jr. You'll find this article at www.ISDESIGNET.com/magazine/apr'96/commentary.html.

How to Use Staff Memos Effectively

The Challenge

Doesn't it seem that there is always something that needs to be said to the entire staff? When I am visiting other centers I can always catch the director reminding somebody to do something.

Solutions

I decided that there were two options:

1. I could have weekly staff meetings, or
2. I could send out Monday memos.

Guess which one I chose? You got it, number two. However, I realize that memos can be missed so I had to be creative when it came to this one. Every Monday I had a memo waiting in staff mailboxes. The memo consisted of many topics: reminders, information, dates, encouragement, and more reminders. I even felt comfortable addressing issues through the Monday Memo. For example, "When I looked outside on Friday, I saw the benches covered with teachers sitting. Don't forget that the children are waiting to see what you can build in the sandbox or how fast you can run." If double reminders are needed, I added a note on the wipe-off board in addition to the Monday Memo.

The Monday memo worked great when teachers read it. But how could I make sure the staff read it? I posted a copy next to the time clock and asked the staff to initial the master copy after they had a chance to read their Monday Memo. On Friday morning, I took down the initialed memo and placed it in a master file. I kept these just in case I needed to address an issue with a staff member that had been covered previously in a memo. If they had initialed the memo, then they could not say they did not know the issue had been mentioned. Sounds boring, huh? It was, so I came up with some better motivation. First, I would include a funny task in the memo. For example, "Tomorrow is Mandy's birthday. Whoever sings 'Happy Birthday' to her or makes her a birthday card can have a piece of her birthday cake." Second, we instituted "Friday Trivia Day." When staff members clocked in on Friday, they saw a question on the wipe-off board based on that week's Monday memo. If the staff member answered the question correctly, he or she received a piece of chocolate or other "goody." The staff really got into these contests, which worked for me because it got them to read their memos!

Key Points to Remember

◆ Start a Monday Memo for the staff. Decide on a format that suits you and your staff.
◆ Include important staff information.
◆ Share reminders and encouragements.
◆ Ask staff to initial a master copy posted near the time clock.

- Include an easy task in the memo and offer a small prize (a sticker is fine).
- Start Friday Trivia Day. Ask a trivia question based on the memo and offer a piece of chocolate to the staff member(s) who answers it correctly.

For More Information

* For complete bibliography, see pages 209-217.

- Read "How Do I Relate and Share Professionally?" by Rhonda Forrest and Nadine McCrea in the Jan/Feb 2002 issue of *Child Care Information Exchange*.

How to Conduct Effective Staff Meetings

The Challenge

People often debate over staff meetings—are they necessary, should they be mandatory, how long should they last, how often should they be scheduled?

Solutions

When I first arrived as the new director of a large center, the staff meetings were held during the day once a week. Half of the staff attended the meeting from 1:00-1:30 and the other half from 1:30-2:00. I believed that having staff meetings this often was unnecessary and the split meetings did not build a team. In fact, staff discussed what was said in one meeting that was not said in the other, and it caused some strife among the group. To solve the problem, I sent out a survey asking the staff for their opinions. I gave them three options:

1. Continue staff meetings the way they are.
2. Have staff meetings once a month.
3. Discontinue staff meetings.

If they did not like any of these ideas, I asked them to suggest another idea. In addition, I asked them to justify their answers by explaining why their solution was best for them and the entire center, and how we could implement their solution. I received a variety of answers, but the majority of the staff wanted to have staff meetings and they wanted to have them once a month. So, that is what we did.

The first Thursday evening of every month we met for approximately two hours. I provided dinner and childcare to eliminate some of the reasons staff could not attend in the evenings. If you don't have the money in the budget to offer dinner and childcare, there are other options. Parents are a great resource. Involving parents gives them a chance to give back to the program. For example, if your center has a 12-month program and you have six classrooms, then ask each classroom of parents to sign up for two staff meetings a year. Some of the parents could provide the dinner and others could provide childcare, if necessary. Another option is to have staff bring a sack dinner and provide an activity in the back of the room for the children. This one is a bit noisy, but it can work. It does depend on how many of the staff need childcare in order to attend the meeting.

I suggest starting meetings by welcoming any new staff members and giving them a round of applause for their scavenger hunt scores (see How to Conduct Staff Orientation, page 13). I will never forget the time I joked with a new staff member that we required all new staff to sing at their first staff meeting. I expected her to look at me in horror, but instead she sang "Row, Row, Row Your Boat." It was so enjoyable that our staff decided to make it a real requirement. One of the members of the new staff's team introduced the new teacher and shared the requirement. If the teacher did not feel comfortable singing to the group, other teachers sang along. This ritual gave new staff members a sense of the team they had joined. Next, I facilitated a team-building game or exercise for about 15 minutes. Afterwards we briefly discussed any business items that needed to be addressed (most of these were covered in the Monday Memo) and then I opened the floor for staff members to address any issues they wished to discuss. As I mentioned in an earlier section, my only requirement was that they have a possible solution to the problem. This usually took 20-30 minutes. Next, I suggested that staff members break into teams with their mentor teacher to discuss issues specific to their age group (40 minutes) and lastly, I had staff break into committees (20 minutes). (Staff committees are explained in How to Design Effective Staff Retreats, page 29).

Distribute an agenda the day before each meeting so that staff are aware of what you hope to accomplish (see Sample Staff Meeting Schedule on Appendix page 177). With this format, staff members know what to expect every time, and they actually prepare and look forward to it. Of course, there are times when you have to deviate from this plan slightly. For example, when we were going through NAEYC accreditation, we spent time each meeting sharing information and discussing the process. Survey your staff and see what is going to work for you.

Key Points to Remember

◆ Survey your staff on their opinions regarding staff meetings.

◆ Review the surveys and make a decision.

◆ Start the meeting with an icebreaker or team-building exercise.

◆ Briefly discuss business items (most of this is covered in Monday Memos, see page 25).

◆ Open the floor for staff members to address issues.

◆ Allow time for teaching teams to meet with their mentor teacher to discuss age-specific issues.

◆ Break into staff committees (more on this in How to Design Effective Staff Retreats below).

For More Information

* For complete bibliography, see pages 209-217.

◆ Read *Early Childhood Workshops That Work* by Nancy Alexander for some great icebreakers and team-building games.

◆ *Child Care Information Exchange* usually includes a training tip in each edition.

◆ Read *The Circle of Influence* by Paula Jorde Bloom.

How to Design Effective Staff Retreats

The Challenge

As a director I had a vision for our program—that it was a place where the staff worked together, focused on providing quality care for the children and support for the parents. Many programs offer great care and support for children and parents, but I wanted to a see a group working together as a team of 30 instead of 30 individuals who happened to work together. I realized that it was not enough for me to have the vision, I also needed the staff to share in this vision.

Solutions

I decided the staff could bond better if we were away from work. I wanted to create an environment that would allow the staff to be themselves, instead of functioning only in their roles as teachers. I looked at my budget to see what I could afford. I called some area conference centers to get an idea about pricing. I found a church conference center about 30 minutes away from our center and we headed there one Friday after the center closed. We arrived in time for dinner and had some team-building time that night. We worked together

on puzzles (made out of developmentally appropriate sayings), and we played old-fashioned relay games (such as three-legged races and raw egg relays) with simple prizes such as candles, bath items, and other small treats I purchased at the local Dollar Store. The staff loved it. I also had a few gift certificates, which we held drawings for later in the evening.

I invited the staff to join me on a walk in the morning before breakfast. It was not mandatory, but about 75% of the staff came. After breakfast the staff were divided into four teams for a scavenger hunt. Some of the items on the hunt included a fork from the dining hall, a signature of a conference staff member, a copy of the school handbook (which no one had), and a sewing kit. There were points associated with each item and the winning team each won a large Hershey's chocolate candy bar. The staff loved the game and the prizes.

We ended the day with a meeting to go over the vision I had for the center and the staff. We were getting ready to go through NAEYC accreditation and I wanted to make sure everyone understood what the process was about and what would be expected of us during and after the process. I definitely played the role of the cheerleader during this meeting. However, I wanted the staff to leave just as fired up about NAEYC as I was. Together we came up with benefits of accreditation, barriers to the process, and ways to knock the barriers down. It was a great retreat. (By the way, the center did get accredited.)

In another program I directed, my budget was a little larger and I had a larger staff so I rented a bed and breakfast in the mountains (about an hour from our center). I know you might think this is too expensive, but it was actually reasonable. We closed our center a few hours early that day, and we took two school vans to the mountains. The administrative staff and I went up the day before to plan and set goals, as well as prepare the environment for the staff's arrival. We put flowers in the rooms and mints on the pillows. The administrative team made "goodie bags" for each staff member. We asked parents to donate the items for the goodie bags. Each class was responsible for bringing 30 of a certain item. We included the following in the goodie bags: gum, candy, fruit, mints, small notebook, pen, lotion, and votive candle. The bags were a huge hit!

The first evening was strictly for team building. We had a family-style dinner and we learned a lot about each other's eating habits and food preferences. I facilitated a team-building activity and gave away lots of door prizes. The night ended with staff members sitting and talking in rocking chairs, enjoying each other's conversation.

The next day was a planning day for the staff. I invited the staff to take a note card (or several note cards) and write down any change they would like to see in our center. Some filled out one card and others filled out five cards. You might be thinking I am crazy for doing this, but keep reading! We separated the cards into categories: parent issues, curriculum issues, benefits and pay issues (that was a big one), classroom issues, space issues, and staff issues. The staff was divided into six groups and asked to take a category. Once each group had a category, they were asked to make a list of the benefits of implementing what was on the

card. Upon completion, they were to pass their category and list to the group on their right. Next, the groups (with their new category) listed the barriers that might prevent the implementation of these cards. Once again, the category was passed upon completion. The third groups looked at their category, weighed the benefits against the barriers, and decided which cards were workable. The workable cards were passed one final time, and the last group created a plan of action for each card.

Once the benefits, barriers, and plan of action were completed, it was time to see who was serious about seeing these changes happen. I told the staff that they would be in charge of these tasks. They decided they needed staff committees, committee chairs, and committee members. Among themselves they decided who would do what on which committee. It was great to watch!

We left that retreat with new committees for the upcoming year. In the past we had a committee here and there for special events, but nothing this organized and with this much focus. These teachers seemed committed to seeing their ideas come to fruition. After we left the retreat, staff members were invited to continue thinking of new ideas that could improve our program or their work environment. When a staff member had a new idea, he or she could give a note card to the committee chair responsible for that category and the committee would consider it. Upon returning to our center, I met with the committee chairs and we decided the committees could meet during staff meeting each month (as mentioned in How to Conduct Effective Staff Meetings, see page 27). This made meetings easy and consistent. It was amazing to see how much these committees were able to accomplish.

The next year rolled around and it was time for our planning weekend. I decided to have a speaker come in for part of our time so I needed to save a little money on our accommodations. I called several hotels and found one that would give us a discount because we were a group of teachers (it never hurts to ask). Friday night had a little more purpose this year. I had the teachers draw names and work in groups with a bag of props that I provided. They had to come up with a group name and slogan and then create a skit using all of the props in the bag. It was a great team-building game. Next, I presented a large canvas and paint to the entire group, but no brushes. I invited the staff to contribute to this artwork that I would later hang in the staff lounge. It was very interesting to watch. Some teachers jumped right in with their fingers while others rolled up paper or used the end of their pen to paint. One staff member even took off his shoe and painted with his toes. The picture turned out beautifully and is still hanging in the staff lounge of the center. Saturday was spent with a few vision exercises and a guest speaker.

After the second year I alternated plans—out-of-town staff retreat one year and in-town meeting with special guest the next. Both cost about the same amount, but it provided a different environment each year. I tried to find new places for our out-of-town trip.

If your budget will simply not allow an overnight trip, this idea can still work. Plan a "retreat"-type meeting one Saturday. Many churches or non-profit organizations will allow you to use their facility. You can still ask parents to donate items for goodie bags and solicit freebies from local businesses. You will be surprised by how much staff members can get out of just being in one room working together without the distractions of day-to-day "center" details.

Key Points to Remember

◆ Decide to have a staff retreat.
◆ Plan your retreat. I suggest team-building on Friday evening and planning and goal setting on Saturday morning.
◆ Get there early to prepare the environment.
◆ Enjoy the retreat!
◆ Evaluate the retreat.
◆ If you can't afford an overnight retreat, meet on a Saturday in a place other than the center for a "retreat" feel.

For More Information

* For complete bibliography, see pages 209-217.

◆ Read *Does Your Team Work Together?* by Roger and Bonnie Neugebauer.
◆ *Games Trainers Play* by John W. Newstrom and Edward Scannell is another good resource.

How to Handle Sensitive Subjects

The Challenge

In any business that involves dealing with people, you will have to address sensitive subjects. I remember one issue that we had to deal with as an entire staff. We had our first set of same-sex parents tour the center. They were getting ready to adopt a daughter, and they wanted to enroll her in our church program. Questions arose among the staff. "How do we handle this?" "What if we don't agree with this lifestyle?" "What do we tell the other families?" "What do we call the parents?"

Solutions

As the director, I was responsible for setting the tone. I decided that we could and would care for this child the same as any other. The issue was not whether any of us agreed or disagreed with the lifestyle of these parents, but whether we could offer this child a quality care experience. I thought we could. As far as how to address these parents, I simply asked them what the child would call them and we did the same. We invited the child to bring in family

pictures just as any other child would. Yes, her family was different, and, yes, we had to be sensitive to that in dealing with her. There are many other sensitive subjects we handle. For eample, when a child is not being bathed, or when a mother yells at her daughter all the way down the hall. How do you deal with these?

We are in a sensitive business. We are not dealing with computers or one-time clients. We are dealing with families, families who might be part of our lives for 5 or even 10 years. In the situations described above, as the director, I would probably handle any discussions with staff members or with the family. I think it is important to protect the relationship that the teachers have with the parents. It is sometimes difficult for teachers to approach parents on tough issues, and I believe that the director should, if the teacher wishes, be willing to take on those issues for the staff.

Key Points to Remember

- You *will* deal with sensitive subjects.
- Look at each issue separately and ask yourself, "What is best for the child?"
- Discuss the issues with only those involved.
- Be willing to step in and support the staff when a sensitive issue arises.

For More Information

* For complete bibliography, see pages 209-217.

- Read *Staff Challenges* by Roger and Bonnie Neugebauer.

What to Do When Staff Do Not Get Along

The Challenge

One morning I ran into the hall to see what all of the screaming was about. There I saw two grown women screaming, shaking fingers, and stomping around. I prayed that the hall would remain free of parents and children until their dispute was settled!

Solutions

I asked the two staff members to move into my office so they could have privacy. I closed the door immediately. After a few minutes and more screaming, I peeked in to see if I could be of some help. They were fighting about the fact that one of them kept leaving the other alone in the classroom.

We sat down and tried to develop a plan. The teacher who had been leaving the classroom said her stomach hurt. We agreed that if she felt sick she probably needed to go home. In the future, the teacher who needed to leave the classroom would ask a member of the administrative team or a floater to stay in her room while she took a break. If no one was

available, she would have to wait. After discussing the situation, they both felt fine, and I was glad that they had reached an amicable solution.

What happens when it does not work out this well? Start with ground rules. Let the staff members know that you expect them to be role models for the children in their care. If they have issues with each other they must find a private place for discussion. Serve as a mediator, if needed. If this continues and you see their disagreements affecting their work, it is time to make a change. If you value both staff members, consider moving one to another position. If not, decide who and what is best for your program and follow through with your plan.

Key Points to Remember

◆ Private communication is essential.
◆ Step in as a mediator, if needed.
◆ Do what's best for the children and for the center.

For More Information

* For complete bibliography, see pages 209-217.

◆ Read "Ways of Talking—Respecting Differences" by Celia Genishi and Anne Haas Dyson and "Resolving Staff Conflict" by Glenn W. Olsen and Steven W. Shirley, two articles from *Child Care Information Exchange.*

How to Use Staff Questionnaires

The Challenge

When I applied to take my first center through NAEYC accreditation, I was horrified that staff questionnaires were a requirement. I had been a director for about six months, and I was a bit insecure about other's opinions of me and my job. Finally, it was deadline time, and I had to send out the questionnaires.

Solutions

It took me several days to get up the nerve to actually read my first completed questionnaire. I thought that I would be shot down, that the staff thought the center and its director (me) were terrible. To my surprise, the questionnaires said neither. In fact, overall, the responses were very good and the issues that staff mentioned in the questionnaires could be addressed.

By the end of the accreditation process, I actually understood the importance of questionnaires. I went from never wanting to ask opinions to asking them often.

I began implementing some type of staff questionnaire (see Sample Yearly Staff Questionnaire on page 178 of the Appendix) on a yearly basis. The actual questionnaire you use can vary from short and sweet with a few basic questions (similar to the one used in How to Help Parents Get to Know Staff on page 88) to the three-page, heavy-duty, multiple-choice questionnaire similar to the one NAEYC has staff complete during the accreditation process. Either way, you are showing your staff that you value their input. Always leave room for comments at the bottom of any questionnaire, inviting staff to write any additional comments. Staff members will feel more comfortable answering a questionnaire honestly if they can do so anonymously.

It is very important to follow up with staff members after the questionnaires have been reviewed. You can provide feedback on the questionnaire at the next staff meeting. The staff in your center will know that you respect their ideas if you take time to consider what they have to say and are willing to make some changes in your program. Of course you will not be able to grant every wish requested. When that is the case, stating some of the reasons you made your decision will assure the staff member(s) that you did consider their ideas.

Key Points to Remember

◆   Offer questionnaires to your staff on a regular basis.
◆   Use a variety of questionnaires.
◆   Let staff know that you take their comments seriously.

For More Information

* For complete bibliography, see pages 209-217.

◆   Read *Growing Teachers: Partnerships in Staff Development* edited by Elizabeth Jones.

How to Conduct Effective Staff Evaluations

The Challenge

Most administrators I know would not rate staff evaluations as a favorite part of their job. In the field of early childhood you will usually find directors who are sensitive, tenderhearted people who do not care for conflict. Therefore, staff evaluations can find themselves on the back burner.

Solutions

I knew that if I wanted to handle staff evaluations better, I had to change my thoughts about them. I needed a new outlook on the evaluation process. I decided to call on a few of my colleagues and get their advice. Finally, I talked to a director with real insight on the subject. She suggested that I approach evaluations as if they were growing experiences, not tests. The following was her approach to the evaluation process:

1. Schedule the staff evaluation.
2. Provide the staff member with a self-evaluation form (see Sample Yearly Staff Evalution on page 179 of the Appendix) two weeks before the scheduled evaluation.
3. Complete the same evaluation form for each staff member who is being evaluated.
4. Prepare the environment. If you cannot take the staff member out for coffee, have coffee and dessert ready in your office or other private area.
5. Review both the staff member's evaluation as well as your own evaluation of the staff member.
6. Set specific goals that address any areas needing improvement.
7. Set specific training goals for the next year.
8. Discuss a pay raise.
9. Finish the evaluation with a positive comment regarding the staff member's job performance.

I thought this plan was definitely worth trying, and it was great! Many staff members shared positive comments about the new evaluation process, and I liked it much better, too.

Key Points to Remember

◆ Follow steps 1-9 on the previous page.

◆ Just do it!

For More Information

* For complete bibliography, see pages 209-217.

◆ Read *Taking Stock* by Roger Neugebauer (editor).

How to Handle Gossip

The Challenge

Gossip, gossip, gossip... people love it. Our society spends millions of dollars every year buying gossip magazines and watching gossip shows on television. If directors had a dollar for every rumor started or passed along in their centers, they would not need to earn salaries!

Solutions

Talking is fun for me. I love to talk, and as a director, I loved to be informed about the latest school issues. However, I preferred that we talk honestly about these issues instead of passing them around in the bathroom or staff lounge. In order to accomplish my goal, I implemented the following "straight talk" ideas:

The Gossip Board and Box—In the staff lounge I hung a big wipe-off board (as mentioned in How to Communicate Effectively on page 23) and wrote on the top, "Stop and Think Before You Share, All Gossip Stops Here!" Staff members were free to write questions and answers about something they'd heard instead of simply passing it around as "fact." It really worked well. If the gossip needed to be addressed by a staff member or myself, it could be done without anyone identifying herself or himself. I also had a locked gossip box (I kept the key) if the gossip was too personal to post. This allowed staff members to write down the gossip they were hearing, and I could address it.

Rumor or Reality—In our staff meetings I gave teachers the opportunity to clear up rumors that were going around. The people mentioned in any rumor would have the chance to clear up the rumor with reality. If the rumor was too personal to address in a staff meeting, teachers were encouraged to go straight to the person involved. These two ideas helped staff members remember that gossiping hurts—it hurts the individuals involved and it hurts the staff as a whole.

Keep in mind that there is a big difference between gossip and useful, helpful information. Here is an example: A staff member (Stephanie) shares with another staff member (Kari) that a parent was upset the night before at pick-up time because her daughter, Maggie, who is in Kari's class,

was filthy and had a scratch. This is useful information because Kari can talk to Maggie's mother and clear things up. However, if Stephanie tells Kari that Maggie's mother was upset because another parent took her parking spot, that is gossip.

I understand that people talk and curiosity tends to get the best of some of us. Of course, I would have preferred for staff members to just stop sharing the rumors, but I was realistic. Sometimes staff members needed help, and these ideas really helped in my center. I think the biggest help of all was honesty. I tended to be very honest about my feelings on gossip and encouraged other staff members to do the same. Once staff members realize that you take this issue seriously, they tend to stop and think before they share. This applies to directors, too.

Key Points to Remember

◆ Acknowledge that gossip is a problem.
◆ Provide a large wipe-off board in the staff lounge entitled the "Gossip Board." Encourage staff to write their gossip questions on the board.
◆ Keep a locked box in the lounge for personal gossip items to be written down.
◆ Provide staff members the opportunity to discuss their gossip issues.
◆ Communication is key; be a role model.

For More Information

* For complete bibliography, see pages 209-217.
◆ Read "Countering Center Gossip" by Margaret Leitch Copeland and Holly Elissa Bruno in the March/April 2001 issue of *Child Care Information Exchange.*

How to Address Burnout

The Challenge

You don't have to work in the field of early childhood for very long before you realize that burnout is all too common among the staff. There are some warning signs of staff burnout: constant complaining, continuously leaving the classroom, showing up late, or not showing up at all.

Solutions

There are many ways to help staff avoid burnout. Offering a lot of support and encouragement worked best for me. The following are some of my favorite ideas for "blowing out" burnout:

1. Provide breaks for staff—Fifteen-minute breaks on a regular basis can do wonders for a staff member's well-being.
2. Provide paid planning time for teachers—It is ideal if both teachers can plan together at least once a week. In order to staff the rooms consistently, consider moving some part-time staff to full-time.
3. Ask parents to help with a teacher appreciation day—Try to schedule a teacher appreciation day at least once per year. Celebrate teachers the entire day. Start with breakfast and end with a nice dinner after work. It is an extra perk to provide transportation to dinner. (I have rented everything from a double-decker bus to a limousine!) Believe me, your budget can handle these events if you are creative, or if you ask for the service to be donated. (The worst thing someone can say is, "No"!) At dinner, we gave away special door prizes that were donated by local businesses and solicited by parents. The teacher appreciation day ended with a small gift check from the center. The teachers reminisced about this night on many occasions.
4. Hire a personal trainer to work out with your staff twice a week—The staff actually foots the bill for this one. (It is quite affordable!) During lunch breaks the teachers can get in a little exercise, which helps reduce their stress levels.
5. Use "Happies" to make staff members happy—Payday is a great time for a "happy." Some of my favorites include PayDay candy bars, appreciation notes, and bagels. However, you certainly don't have to wait until payday to pass out goodies. Just keeping a bowl of Hershey's Hugs and Kisses in your office can help staff in need of a chocolate break.
6. Take the time to notice—Teachers really appreciate hearing about the good things going on in their classroom. When you compliment a teacher, be specific. For example, "Jenny, I peeked in your room this morning and watched the children pretend to make you breakfast. You were really engaged with them and I could hear their giggles all the way down the hall. You created memories for those children today and I just wanted to say thanks." This says to the teacher that he or she is important enough for you to observe and

share your observation with him or her.

7. Arrange tours of other centers— Try to schedule tours of other quality centers for the staff to visit. It is a nice change for them to get out of their own environment and see how other teachers facilitate their classrooms. Staff members usually come back with some new ideas and a renewed spirit. Many parents are willing to fill in for an hour or two in their child's classroom to provide teachers this opportunity.

8. Encourage staff to get a hobby—Acknowledge that it is important to balance work and play. For example, some of my hobbies are playing tennis, baking bread, and watching a good movie with my husband.

9. Recognize special events—When a teacher has a baby, gets his CDA, or is on time four weeks in a row, take notice. This can be as simple as a congratulations card or a pack of diapers.

10. Encourage growth—Many staff experience burnout because they feel that they are stagnating as professionals. Encourage interested staff to stretch themselves by getting involved in a local early childhood organization, applying for a mentoring position, developing a training workshop and submitting a proposal to a conference, or writing an article for a professional magazine. Most of the time, we just need someone to gently push us in the right direction.

Key Points to Remember

◆   Acknowledge that burnout is an issue in the field of early childhood education.

◆   Read the above ideas and try them out.

◆   Come up with more ideas.

For More Information

* For complete bibliography, see pages 209-217.

◆   Read "Who's Caring for Caregivers" by Karen Petty in the Summer 1999 issue of *Texas Child Care.*

◆   Check out the website www.motivateteachers.com.

How to Notice the Good Things and Express Your Gratitude

The Challenge

Saying "thank you" is part of basic good manners, but more important, it makes people feel good to know you noticed something and appreciated it. It is important for directors to notice and appreciate the good things that staff members are doing in their program.

Solutions

We thanked the staff at our center in several ways:

◆ Teacher Appreciation Breakfast—Once a month, the parents (one classroom per month) provided breakfast for the staff. Some months the parents donated money for donuts and coffee, and other months parents made breakfast casseroles and muffins. Either way, the staff members were grateful. It was a fun way for parents to say, "Thank you."

◆ Thank-You Notes—Teachers, staff, and children were encouraged to send thank-you notes to those who needed them. Staff had mailboxes in the office where notes could be left. I tried to write each staff member throughout the year to say thanks!

◆ Staff Member of the Month—This was an award that was chosen by the staff. Staff had to write down their nomination and a specific reason why they felt that staff member should be chosen. We listed the nominees, the winner, and the kind words in the staff Monday Memo (see page 25). The staff member of the month received a half day off during the next month (feel free to choose your own prize).

◆ Saying Thanks—It is important as a director to take the time to express your gratitude when appropriate. People never get tired of those two little words: THANK YOU!

◆ Teacher Appreciation Committee—The parents were also responsible for this one. During the year, this committee would come together to provide small gifts for the staff members. Whether it was candy, an apron painted with the children's handprints, or coupons for lunch, this committee really went the extra mile.

Key Points to Remember

◆ Be purposeful about showing appreciation.

◆ Provide a Teacher Appreciation Breakfast once a month.

◆ Write thank-you notes.

◆ Choose a Staff Member of the Month.

◆ Encourage parents to start a Teacher Appreciation Committee.

For More Information

* For complete bibliography, see pages 209-217.

◆ Look up www.education-world.com/a_admin/admin162.shtml or www.firstschool.com/activities/occasions/teachers.htm for ideas.

◆ *101 Great Gifts From Kids* by Stephanie Mueller and Ann Wheeler is a great book of ideas for children to use to make unique gifts for parents and other important people in their lives. Wouldn't it be fun to turn the tables and ask the parents and children to make great gifts for the teachers?

How to Create a Community by Making Memories With the Staff

The Challenge

Making memories with the staff in your center is an important part of the "community feeling" directors should be developing. By displaying some of the evidence of memories, you convey to the staff their importance. It also gives prospective parents a glimpse at what their child might experience in your program.

Solutions

Memory Masterpiece—Each year the staff members created art to display around the center. I would usually buy a large canvas and some bright paints for the staff and let them decide what to create. They were not allowed to write words, other than their signature, and everyone had to participate. I wrote the date on the masterpiece and hung the newest one close to the entry of the center. This is a super, inexpensive way to decorate the hallway of your center and display your memories!

Photos—I am a photo fanatic! I have photos all over my home, and my center was no exception. Do you have photo albums and framed pictures throughout your center? If not, I suggest adding them as soon as possible. Ask if anyone wants to be the official staff photographer. Encourage him or her to take pictures during all staff functions (make sure he or she gets in some of the pictures). During our bigger events, such as teacher appreciation day or staff retreat, I passed around several disposable cameras for the staff to use. I developed the film and transferred the photos into frames and albums. This was a great, economical way for the parents and children to see the staff in arenas other than their classrooms. This was especially fun for children because most of them think the staff members live at the center. I also used the photo albums to show prospective teachers the camaraderie of our staff. Pictures really do say a thousand words.

Storytelling—Encourage staff to write down stories that stick out throughout their day. I often share the stories in the staff memo and occasionally in the parent newsletter.

Take the time to say good-bye—When a staff member leaves your center, take the time to give him or her a memory of some sort.

I still have several of the memory tokens that were given to me when I left my last director's job. One parent gave me a special book, one teacher gave me a pair of earrings, and one child made me a special picture. The parent committee organized a plan to have each child contribute artwork, and they also presented me with a set of pottery dishes that I still use. I think of those children, staff, and parents each time I pull out one of the coffee mugs or plates. When someone leaves a program for whatever reason, memories will go with them. Help provide something tangible, such as a personal photo album or coffee mug with handprints.

Key Points to Remember

- Encourage staff to create a Memory Masterpiece.
- Take a lot of photos of staff and display them around the center.
- Encourage the staff to share stories.
- Share memories with staff when it is time to say goodbye.

For More Information

* For complete bibliography, see pages 209-217.

- Read the article "Preserving Memories: A Blueprint for Teachers" in the Spring 2000 issue of *Dimensions of Early Childhood.*

Challenges Related to Children

How to Help Teachers Understand the Difference Between a Child-Centered and Teacher-Directed Curriculum

The Challenge

Helping teachers understand the difference between a child-directed and a teacher-directed classroom environment could be one of the biggest challenges you face. I remember walking down the hall of a center as the new director and hearing a teacher say, "Alex, I am going to hold your hand and help you put the glue on your picture. Your mommy wants this cow to be pretty so she can hang it on her refrigerator." I knew I had a challenge ahead of me.

Solutions

Helping teachers make the change to a child-directed curriculum is a challenge for several reasons. First, the teacher has a valid point about the parents. Many parents do expect "pretty" art projects every night. Next, the teacher has probably been offering art experiences like these for some time and may not see the need for change. Third, when

47

some staff hear "child-directed" they think that they can sit back and relax while the children run free. They don't understand their role.

First, I decided to observe in each classroom. After I had a better feel for what the staff understood about a child-centered environment, I set some goals for the following year. Yes, I gave myself a full year to help move the staff and the center to a curriculum that offered child-directed activities on a daily basis. I considered this a process. As a director, I had made the mistake of walking into classrooms and demanding changes, but with experience, I learned that it is worth the wait to educate the teachers about the benefits of a child-directed classroom environment. Why? Because I wanted them to WANT to make the change, and not feel like they were being forced.

What was my plan? At our next staff meeting, I introduced the subject with the "airplane game." I divided the staff into two groups and had them sit at tables on separate sides of the room. The assistant director, who was helping to facilitate the meeting, instructed one group on how to make paper airplanes. The staff was to follow her directions exactly. All the staff members on this side of the room made the same paper airplane. Meanwhile, on the other side of the room, I displayed pictures of real airplanes, model

airplanes, and toy airplanes. I provided teachers with a variety of materials and invited them to make an airplane. I walked around acknowledging their work and answering questions. Guess what? We each made completely different airplanes. After the activity I asked the group, "What are the benefits to offering the second type of activity over the first?" and "What are the barriers to offering the second type of activity over the first?" In a learning situation, the benefits usually affect the children and the barriers usually impact the adults.

This situation was no different. The teachers immediately said that making the creative airplane was more individual, but some parents would not even know it was an airplane, or that making the creative airplane was more fun, but the other one was easier to clean up. Each barrier had to be addressed. To help the staff solve these issues, I asked them how they would handle the barriers. My experience has been that if people can find a way to deal with potential problems, they are more willing to try something new.

Next, I scheduled a staff training session at another center with a well-known speaker who focused on how to provide a child-centered environment. I felt that this would give some credibility to what I was saying because they would hear it from someone other than me. Because I was sharing the cost with several other programs, this staff training was not very expensive. This is a great way to bring in speakers who can focus on your needs, but not break your budget. This training made a real difference. The staff really connected with this speaker, and they began to see a need for change.

Another way I worked towards my goal was with new staff. I tried very hard to hire new staff members who already embraced a child-centered philosophy and could immediately implement it in their classroom. This helped others get excited because they noticed something different in these classrooms and were intrigued to find out more.

Role modeling is really effective when trying to get staff members to see the importance of what you are saying. There are many ways to model a child-centered philosophy to your staff:

◆ Have a teacher with a child-centered curriculum invite another teacher into his or her room for the morning (provided a substitute can be found).

◆ Work with another center that is willing to allow your staff to come in and observe for the day. This one works extremely well because your teachers can observe other teachers teaching the same age group. This shows your staff how to make it work with their particular age group, and it also gives them a colleague they can call for advice.

How do you help staff members understand the role of the teacher in a child-centered classroom? The way I see it, most teachers who have a teacher-directed classroom tend to control the room and teachers who have a child-centered classroom facilitate the room. When we were preparing for a training one day, a friend and I came up with the following poem. Feel free to use it with your staff.

The Facilitating Teacher
By Kathy Lee and Carole Dibble

The controller makes the choices,
The facilitator allows for choice.

The controller knows the answers,
The facilitator asks the questions.

The controller makes the decisions,
The facilitator leads in decision making.

The controller provides the model,
The facilitator provides the inspiration.

The controller demands obedience,
The facilitator inspires respect.

The controller dictates with rules,
The facilitator allows ideas to dictate.

Dare to be a facilitator, not a controller.

A great activity to take this poem a step further is to break your staff into groups and have them come up with additional lines for the poem. Put it all together and create your own version to post in the staff lounge or office as a reminder. However, I encourage you to be sensitive when you share this poem. Let your staff know that we have all been controllers and that there are still times when a situation needs to be controlled. For example, if one child is hitting another child, it is not the time to sit back and let them "work it out." It always helps when staff members understand that you have "been there." Tell staff members that the authors of that poem have been both controllers and facilitators. I can count too many times when I chose to control a situation instead of facilitate it. Most of the time, I regretted it later.

Another way to help them understand their role is through role-playing exercises. In a staff meeting, prepare some common classroom scenarios, such as children taking toys from other children, using inappropriate language, or refusing to participate in an activity, and ask the teachers to role play the situations first as a controlling teacher and then as a facilitating teacher. It is really a fun exercise and gets the point across nicely.

A related issue is when parents don't understand the importance of the process of learning versus the product of learning. Sometimes parents like a product because it says, "My child did something today." If teachers work hard at communicating what happens in the room each day (through pictures, notes, and verbal communication), parents will better accept a process-oriented, child-directed classroom. For more on this topic, see page 106, How to Deal With the Academically Minded Parent.

I have included some child-centered curriculums in the For More Information section below. Tell your staff that even though there are many great curriculums available, they should get to know the children in their classroom and base activities on the children's needs. Prospective parents always asked me what curriculum we used in our center and I always responded, "The children are our curriculum. When your child enters our program, our curriculum will have to change to make sure we are meeting all of his or her needs." When we focus on the children and ask ourselves, "Is it good for them?", we will make the right decisions and we will have a child-centered program.

Key Points to Remember

- Look at the act of moving your center towards a child-centered curriculum as a process.
- Address each barrier that may come with moving towards a child-centered approach.
- Have the staff observe other teachers and role play.

For More Information

* For complete bibliography, see pages 209-217.

- Attend a local, state, or national early childhood conference.
- Possible approaches/curriculums to use include:
    Bank Street
    Creative Curriculum

High Scope
Innovations
NAEYC Developmentally Appropriate Practices
Reggio Emilia

How to Learn Children's Names

The Challenge

One of the most overwhelming jobs as a director is learning the names of the children. I'll never forget the day that I proudly called a little boy by the wrong name. He corrected me, but did I learn his name? No! I continued calling this boy by the wrong name for weeks. His face showed his discouragement with me.

Solutions

There are all sorts of tricks for remembering names. Some people suggest associating something with the person that will remind you of his or her name. The trick that works best for me is to make eye contact (that means getting down to the child's level) with the person I am meeting, and then repeating the person's name several times during that first conversation.

Determine a goal. You might want to focus on learning the names of the children in two classrooms per week until you have learned all of the children's names. Visit the classrooms regularly and try to name every child present. Later in the day, look at the class roll and visualize each child. If you can't see certain faces in your mind, go back to the classroom and visit with that child. It does take time, but you will succeed. If you do forget, don't pretend to remember. Just as we tell the children, it is always okay to ask for help.

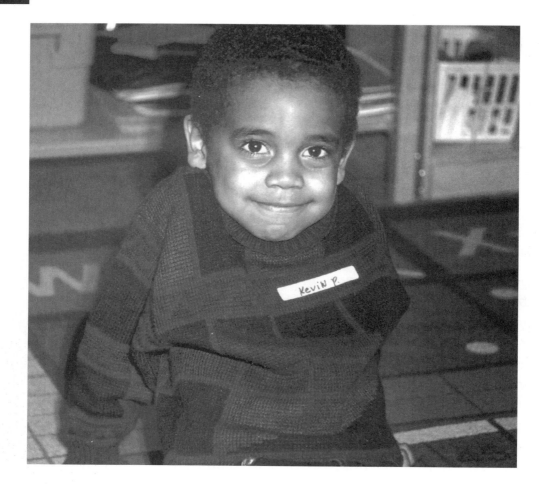

Key Points to Remember

◆ Get down on the child's level and make eye contact when you meet a child for the first time.

◆ Use the child's name several times during this first meeting.

◆ Visit the child's classroom on a regular basis to check your memory.

◆ If you forget, just ask—children are very forgiving.

For More Information

* For complete bibliography, see pages 209-217.

◆ Read *The Complete Idiot's Guide to Improving Your Memory* by Michael Kurland and Richard A. Lupoff and *Total Memory Workout* by Cynthia R. Green, PhD.

◆ Check out the website www.learnthat.com/courses/lifestyle/names.

Why Greeting Children Is Important

The Challenge

The morning role of a director can be challenging—dealing with teachers calling in sick, children arriving, parents asking questions, and other issues that always pop up. What is a director to do? In my center, the children would walk by my office and say hello, but many times, I was too busy to respond. I felt badly about this and wanted the children to feel at home, so I needed a plan.

Solutions

During a session at a wonderful early childhood education conference, a facilitator of one workshop gave me the answer to my dilemma. She explained that as children entered her center she greeted them with, "I have been waiting for you." Well, I loved it! The next day I decided to try it out at my center. I noticed that after greeting the children for a short period they got used to me greeting them every morning. One morning I walked into a classroom and one little boy said, "Here I am! I know you have been waiting for me." Obviously, I had not greeted him that morning, but he knew I wouldn't forget him. It confirmed to me that greeting time was an important and sacred time.

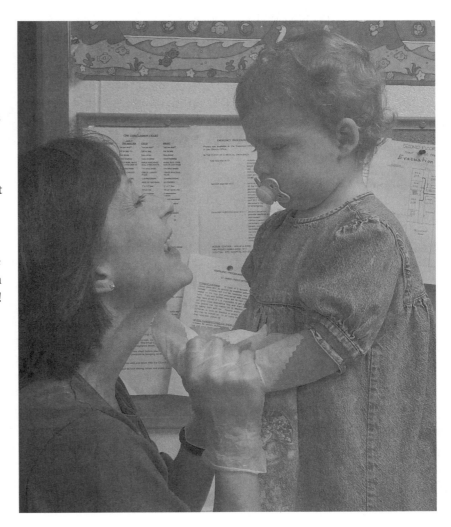

In addition to the children feeling important, the parents took note of my greeting. When I knelt down, greeted, and sometimes hugged the children, my actions told parents, "This child is important here." I am convinced it helped many parents go to work feeling more confident about the care their child would receive that day.

I began to value this time so much that I adjusted my schedule so meetings would not occur until after drop-off time. Eventually, I asked a staff member to come in early and help in the office during heavy drop-off time. I never regretted it! If you can't spend the money on extra staff, try using a cordless phone, a headset, or a pager. Think of creative ways to free up your time during the busy drop-off times. If you regularly work at closing time, then also focus on a good-bye message to the children and their families. The point is, as the director, you set the tone for the children and their parents. Let them know you value them as a part of your center "family."

Key Points to Remember

- Plan to greet children in the hallways every morning. (If you are also around when your center closes, then saying good-bye works, too.)
- Tell the children you have been waiting for them, looking out the windows for them, waiting for their car to drive up, or another phrase that is meaningful to you and communicates that the children are important to you.
- Ask a staff member to come in early to help out in the office, or find other ways to free up your time during drop-off and pick-up times.
- Be prepared for children to look for you if you miss them during drop-off time.
- Set the tone for the children and parents.

For More Information

* For complete bibliography, see pages 209-217.

- For feedback on the effectiveness of this approach and/or to gather information about how to change your approach, consider the following:
- Ask the children in the program: "Who do you think I am, and what do you think I do?" Their answers will provide clues as to what approach you should take.
- During your next parent survey (see Sample Yearly Parent Survey on page 183 in the Appendix), ask parents for feedback on the greeting (or the farewell) their children receive from you each day.

How to Determine the Director's Role in the Classroom

The Challenge

As the director of your program, staff and parents may view you as the expert in many areas. Parents may assume you know everything about parenting, even if you have no children of your own. Teachers may assume you are the "perfect" classroom teacher, and children may assume you live at the center. So, what is your role in the classroom?

Solutions

I struggled with this issue before I developed what I call "classroom time." Every morning, after greeting time, I would walk the halls of the center and visit classrooms. I tried to avoid circle time, but snack or center time worked fine. I made a point of walking into every classroom and staying for a few minutes. If a child needed a shoe tied, I would tie it. If a child needed a hug, I would hug him or her. I tried not to interrupt the mood of the classroom, but instead blend in for five minutes or more. It would take about an hour every morning to accomplish this, and there were days I did not get to every classroom.

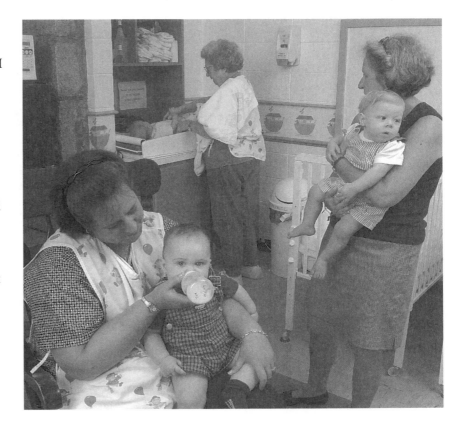

If you are committed to classroom time, everyone feels important. The staff, parents, and children all enjoy seeing the director in the room at some point during the day. Taking time to visit the rooms also helps you get a better picture of what is really happening in your center. Directors who visit classrooms can anticipate classroom issues because they have a greater awareness of the dynamics and challenges.

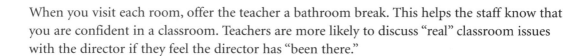

When you visit each room, offer the teacher a bathroom break. This helps the staff know that you are confident in a classroom. Teachers are more likely to discuss "real" classroom issues with the director if they feel the director has "been there."

Key Points to Remember

◆ Schedule time to visit classrooms.
◆ Stop in at a convenient time for the class.
◆ Offer the staff a bathroom break when you go in.
◆ If necessary, model developmentally appropriate practices with the children while you are in a classroom.

For More Information

* For complete bibliography, see pages 209-217.

◆ Talk about these visits during a staff meeting. What would the staff like you to offer during this time? Make sure the time you have scheduled is convenient for them.
◆ Talk with other directors. How do they handle classroom visits? If you are not part of a director's network, check out an early childhood website or listserv. (See a list of websites on page 212.) Ask a question about how to handle classroom visits and you may receive some helpful tips and insights.

How to Handle Discipline

The Challenge

One of the many hats you wear as the director is that of problem solver. Teachers will look to you especially to provide solutions to discipline issues. As long as children are in group care, there will be discipline issues. As long as teachers are in the classroom with the children, you will be asked to "fix" the problem.

Solutions

This is a tough one. Because every child is different and every situation is different, there is no one perfect solution. When a teacher would approach me with a discipline issue (not just a one-time incident), I would ask her or him to keep a journal. Whenever possible, I would observe in the classroom to get a better feel for the situation. Even if I did not observe the specific problem, the teachers felt that my presence indicated that the discipline issue was important to me and that I was making an effort to help them. If my observation and the teacher's observation and insight pointed to a pattern, a certain time of day, or a certain situation that set off the child, the teacher and I discussed possible solutions.

For example, a four-year-old child enrolled in my program had fits of rage throughout the day. I asked the teacher to write journal entries describing the situations surrounding his fits. Through observation, the teacher discovered that the child was reacting to the fact that his mother was a teacher in another classroom. He would see her, but not be able to hug her or talk to her throughout the day. Whenever he saw his mother, he was overcome with anger. We met with his mother and together we came up with a possible solution. The child's teacher started scheduling "mommy time" for this little boy, and it made a tremendous change in his behavior. He knew that there were scheduled times throughout the day that he could spend with his mom, and he could anticipate those times. The plan really worked! Not every situation will have a solution that is this easy, but observing the child to determine whether there is a pattern and developing a plan based on those observations are key components to a successful resolution of the problem.

As the director, you are a resource and a guide. If the staff does not feel support from you in this area, they will struggle. There will be times when you have to be the one to talk with the parents of a child who just can't keep his or her hands to him- or herself, or the one who has to call a parent to say that his or her child has been bitten for the third time (more on biting later). Both are difficult situations, and sometimes, as directors, we need to take the heat for staff.

If you have worked with your staff on a discipline issue and it just isn't getting better, invite the parents in for a brainstorming session. Parents know their children best, and they might have insight that you don't have. Remind the parents that you are addressing this situation together and that you both want what is best for their child. Address the *issue* (biting, hitting, or any other problem behavior) as the problem, not the child! Keep in mind that parents can sometimes be very sensitive when it comes to their children. After discussing the issue, make plans and write them down. Agree to meet again with the teacher and parents to re-visit the issue in two weeks and assess progress made, if any.

If necessary, the next step is to seek professional help from a play therapist, children's counselor, or other appropriate professional. Many times, these professionals will work directly with the center to help remedy the situation. It is a good idea to go ahead and research the professional help available in your area before you need it. Individually, invite the professionals into your center. Get to know them and their philosophy regarding young children. Then, when you need to make a referral, you will be prepared to make a decision that is in the child's best interest.

As a last resort, all involved might conclude that group care is not the best place for that child at that point in his or her life. In my years as a director, I suggested alternative arrangements for only one child. The parents thanked me later, agreeing that an environment with fewer children was better for their child.

Key Points to Remember

◆ Be available for teachers and parents to discuss discipline issues with you.
◆ Encourage teachers to observe a child and keep a journal to discover if a pattern exists in a child's behavior.
◆ Make a plan to conduct a formal observation in that classroom.
◆ Focus on the *behavior* of the child.
◆ Brainstorm with the teachers and parents of the child.
◆ Try different discipline techniques that are appropriate for the issue.
◆ Seek professional help if needed.

For More Information

* For complete bibliography, see pages 209-217.

◆ Stay current on developmentally appropriate discipline techniques by attending local, state, and national early childhood conferences.
◆ Invite an early childhood trainer into your center for a guidance workshop.
◆ Consider the following books:
  But They Spit, Scratch, and Swear by Mary Steiner Whelan
  Conscious Discipline by Becky Bailey
  The Peaceful Classroom by Charles Smith
  The Values Book by Pam Schiller and Tamera Bryant
◆ Surf the web for possible answers. (See a list of websites on page 212.)
◆ Call a local, trusted pediatrician's office for professional referrals. Many churches and schools also have licensed counselors on staff.

How to Handle Special-Needs Children

The Challenge

There will be times in your center when you need to address the issue of children with special needs. This happened in my program. We had a baby who looked like every other baby when she entered the program—adorable! After a few months, the teachers noticed that this baby was not developing along the typical child development lines. She was not holding her head up, trying to crawl, and so on.

Solutions

After meeting with the teachers who had charted the child's development, we decided it was time to approach the parents. We wanted to be careful not to scare or offend them, so we thought it would be best if I met with the parents. I started by asking the parents when their daughter had her last checkup and how it went. The parents did not mention that the doctor had any concerns. I pulled out my developmental checklist (see Sample Developmental Checklists on page 184 in the Appendix) and showed them where their daughter was. I suggested that they take the checklist to their pediatrician and get his or her input. The parents did as I suggested, and the pediatrician referred the parents to a specialist who diagnosed the child as having cerebral palsy. We were able to work with the child's therapists and continue caring for that child.

An important consideration in this situation (and many other situations) is that we must be careful not to make assumptions or judgments. Be professional and offer objective information about the child. Do not attempt to diagnose the situation. Leave that to other professionals. Share the information you know to be true and work with the parents to find answers. Suggesting that the parents take the information to the child's pediatrician is always a good start.

Having a clear policy in place before an issue emerges is essential. Make sure an attorney checks your policy to ensure that it follows the American Disabilities Act. One of the keys to being a successful director is to anticipate the possible scenarios you might face. Having a policy regarding special-needs children in place (see Sample Special Needs Policy on page 189 in the Appendix) will save you some headaches if you ever find yourself in the middle of an emotional meeting regarding a child in your center. Make sure each staff member reads and understands the policy. You might want to include this subject and review your policy at the next staff meeting to ensure everyone is on the same page.

Everyone wants what is best for the child involved. Remember, parents want to think their child is "perfect." Shattering that dream with reality can be tough. Always be sensitive and compassionate. Encourage teachers to try to stand in the parent's shoes when they approach this subject. Be thankful for the specialists that you can call on when you need them. If it gets to the point that your program can no longer meet the child's needs, be honest with the parents and support them as they try to find a new situation for their child.

Key Points to Remember

◆   Be careful not to "diagnose" children, just note the facts.
◆   Make sure the information you discuss is kept confidential.
◆   Encourage the parents to discuss the issue with their child's pediatrician.
◆   Follow up with parents.
◆   Make a plan regarding the future care of this child in your program.
◆   If necessary, ask parents to sign a release form so doctors and therapists can discuss the child with you.
◆   Support staff during any adjustments they might have to make in their classroom.
◆   Be honest with the parents if the time comes that the child needs to be referred to a new program.

For More Information

* For complete bibliography, see pages 209-217.

◆   Research the American Disabilities Act on the web at www.usdoj.gov/crt/ada/adahom1.htm.
◆   Check out the National Information Center for Children and Youth with Disabilities at www.nichcy.org.
◆   Consider the following books:
  Assessing Young Children by Gayle Mindes, Harold Ireton, and Carol Mardell-Czudnowski
  By the Ages: Behavior & Development of Children Prebirth Through 8 by K. Eileen Allen and Lynn R. Marotz

How to Handle Children on Special Diets

The Challenge

I remember my first conversation with a parent who was raising her child as a vegetarian. She told me that she would be bringing in all of her daughter's food, and we were not to allow the child to eat anything in our program.

Solutions

As a director, I often had to handle requests relating to food. Sometimes, the food limitations were based on a belief system, such as being a vegetarian or practicing a religion that has laws governing what people can eat. Other times, it was because the child was allergic or had sensitivities to certain foods. The first thing I did was discuss the issue with the parents, and then, as best as I could, I would make special arrangements for the child.

Using the above instance as an example, I would first attempt to serve the child a vegetarian substitute through our regular meal services. First, I would invite the parent into my office to go over our four-week rotation menu. I would ask the parent to suggest possible vegetarian alternatives that would be similar to the main dish offered. Then I would review the menu with our cook and attempt to put into place a vegetarian substitute for this child and others. Next, I would send the vegetarian menus to our licensing representative to make sure that they met all standards regarding nutrition. Lastly, I would inform the parents that they might incur an additional food fee if our food budget increased due to the added vegetarian alternatives.

If this approach failed for any reason, I would allow the child to bring a lunch from home as long as the guidelines on the following page were met:

1. The parent provided a four-week rotation menu.
2. The menu was submitted to licensing for approval.
3. The child put her food on a plate so the "family style" meal was not disrupted.
4. A written letter from the parents was placed in the child's file stating the fact that the parents were rearing this child as a vegetarian.

When the children ask why a particular child is eating something different, teachers might say, "Whitney's parents say that her tummy needs that food, and your parents say that your tummy needs the food on your plate. Isn't it great that our mommies and daddies know what our tummies need!"

Key Points to Remember

◆ Remember that parents are not trying to make your life difficult; they really have their child's best interest in mind.
◆ Ask the parents if they have solutions to the issue.
◆ Attempt to offer a vegetarian menu alongside your "regular" menu.
◆ Simply tell the children the truth, for example, "Whitney's parents say that Whitney's tummy needs this food, and your parents say that your tummy needs that food." Leave it at that.
◆ A positive attitude will take you a long way.

For More Information

* For complete bibliography, see pages 209-217.

◆ Visit the American School Food Service Association website at www.asfsa.org.
◆ Check out the following books:
    Do Carrots Make You See Better? by Julie Appleton, Nadine McCrea, & Carla Patterson
    Taming of the C.A.N.D.Y. Monster, Continuously Advertised Nutritionally Deficient Yummies: A Cookbook by Vicki Lansky
    Safety, Nutrition, and Health in Child Care by Cathie Robertson
◆ Call your local Home Extension Office for nutrition brochures, posters, and other food- and nutrition-related information.

What to Do When Children Are Sick

The Challenge

One morning, as I was leaving the center to go buy supplies, a teacher with a sick child stopped me. The child and I went back to my office to take her temperature; it was 101.8. In addition, the child was complaining of a stomachache. I called the parents and explained that they had to take the child home because our policy was that a child must not attend the center with a fever greater than 100.4 when other symptoms are present and must remain fever-free, without fever-reducing medicine, for 24 hours before returning. The next morning as I greeted the children, I saw this child and her mother walking through the door.

Solutions

I said, "Good morning, Grace. I am surprised to see you back at school this morning." Her mom said that Grace's fever went down and that her stomach felt fine when they got home. I gave in and let Grace come to school. BIG MISTAKE! You can guess what happened around 11:00 that morning. Grace began to feel sick again. I called Grace's mom. This time when we sent Grace home with her mother, I gave her mother a copy of our sick-child policy (see Sample Sick Policy on page 190 in the Appendix), and asked that Grace's mom abide by the policy.

Having a clear policy that everyone understands is imperative. There are so many different opinions on when a child is most contagious and should be excluded from care. Do your homework and make a decision that you feel is best for the families enrolled in your center. Share your policy with teachers and parents and make sure everyone understands it. Remind parents that your goal is to create the safest environment for all the children in the program.

I quickly learned from my mistake with Grace. After this incident, I began requiring a doctor's note stating that the child could return to school before he or she was free of fever or other symptoms for 24 hours. It really helped. When a parent said, "My son felt better so we thought he should be at school," I would simply say, "Great, just have your doctor's office fax over a statement saying he is okay to be here."

Teachers play a role every morning as they greet the children. Ask the staff to conduct a discreet health check on every child. When the child enters the classroom, the teacher gets down on the child's level to say hello. At that time, they can look for any unusual rashes, check the child's eyes, feel the skin, and ask the child any appropriate questions. This will help catch some symptoms that indicate that the child should return home. This will help your center attempt to eliminate unnecessary spreading of germs. In addition, remind teachers about the importance of hand washing. There are many sources you can use to purchase reminder posters, including school supply stores and catalogs.

Once a child is sent home, as the director, log the sickness in a sick journal. This can be a blank book used only for this purpose, sheets of paper on a clipboard, or sheets of paper stapled together. For each instance, include the following information:

1. the child's symptoms
2. fever (if any)
3. time and date the child left the center, due to illness
4. date the child returns
5. any additional information shared by the parents regarding their child's illness

Keep this journal for at least three months before beginning a new one. This journal is an invaluable help in case any communicable diseases arise or to track the spread of viruses and other germs. If you ever find yourself needing to report an illness to the Centers for Disease Control (CDC), this journal will be extremely helpful.

Key Points to Remember

◆ Review your sick policy and make sure it is up to date.
◆ Inform parents and teachers of your policy.
◆ Keep a sick child in the office or sick room until a parent arrives.
◆ Upon pick-up, hand parents a copy of your sick policy.
◆ Make a note of the child's symptoms in a sick journal.
◆ Discreetly check the child for obvious signs of health (or continued sickness) upon return to school.

For More Information

* For complete bibliography, see pages 209-217.

◆ Visit the National Resource Center for Health and Safety in Child Care website at www.nrc.uchsc.edu. This website offers a wealth of information on this subject and many others.

◆ Parent information regarding health can be found at www.childhealthonline.org/parents.htm

◆ Check out this site — www.cdc.gov/ncidod/hip/abc/intro.htm

◆ Ask a pediatrician a question on www.healthykids.com.

◆ Invite a pediatrician to come and talk with the parents and staff in your center. Make sure it is a pediatrician you know and trust or is known by someone you trust.

◆ Look in school supply stores and catalogs for health-related information.

◆ Take photographs of the children doing each step of the hand washing routine and make your own poster. Use a color copier to make multiple copies to use in all classrooms.

How to Handle Children With Allergies

The Challenge

As a director and parent, I have had experiences with both staff and children and allergies. In one instance, a staff member walked into a room where peanut butter playdough was being made and she immediately broke into hives. On other occasions, we had similar experiences with several children in our center.

Solutions

I believe that peanut butter should be banned from group situations for children. I know it is a favorite of many (including me), but the risk is too great. However, peanut butter is not the only allergen you must consider. Other common ones are soy products and milk. Allergies of any kind are serious; lives are at stake. The staff in every room MUST be informed of allergies in their room. Designate an area in the classroom (the same for each room) to post an allergy list. By doing so, substitutes and special teachers will have access to the information on which children have allergies. It is imperative that staff be trained on spotting allergic reactions in children. Appropriate first aid training should also be conducted in using a child's prescription epi-pen for emergency situations. Whenever children are tasting new foods not posted on the menu, it is always safe practice to send a note to parents the day before with a sign that says, "Allergy Alert: We will be tasting _____ today (date). Please let us know if your child is allergic to _____."

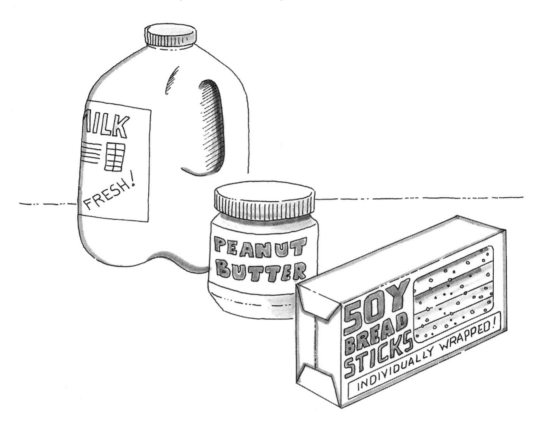

In the infant room, I suggest you ask parents to introduce new foods at home. For example, once the child has tried sweet potatoes at home (without an allergic reaction), the parents can bring sweet potatoes for school. Remind parents that food items such as strawberries, honey, and peanut butter should not be offered before the age of one. Some pediatricians are suggesting that peanut butter be held off until the child reaches age two to cut down on possible allergic reactions. It is important for teachers to write down all foods that an infant consumes and give this list to the parents as a referral for the night. This food record is essential if a child breaks out into hives on the way home and parents need to know what the infant consumed.

Key Points to Remember

- Consider banning peanut butter in your program.
- Inform staff of allergies in their classroom.
- Post allergy signs in a designated area for substitutes to see.
- Train staff in spotting allergic reactions.
- Train staff in first aid procedures for allergic reactions.
- Post tasting signs for parents.
- Encourage parents of young children to introduce new foods at home.

For More Information

* For complete bibliography, see pages 209-217.

- Check out these allergy websites:
  www.spindlepub.com/kids/library/allergy.htm
  www.cchs.net/health/getcontents.asp?DOCID=center&cID=1
- Consider including the following children's books about allergies:
  Allie the Allergic Elephant: A Children's Story of Peanut Allergies by Nicole Smith
  Taking Food Allergies to School by Ellen Weiner and Moss Freedman
- Consider adding the following book to your parent library:
  The Complete Allergy Book by June Engel and Isolde Prince

(See Essential Books for Parent Library on page 191 in the Appendix for a complete list of books that parents might want to have at home.)

What to Do About Dispensing Medicine

The Challenge

Where there are children, there is medicine. Whether it is Triaminic, Amoxil, or Propulsid, parents will want staff to dispense medicine to their children.

Solutions

Start with your school policy regarding medicine (see Sample Policy Concerning Dispensing Medicine on page 192 in the Appendix). It is crucial that center policy be clear. You must decide what is appropriate for your program, complying with local and state licensing standards.

I decided to dispense prescription medicine only. This eliminated parents wanting us to give cold and fever medicines to their children on a regular basis. Before we stopped dispensing non-prescription medicines we often had 25 requests, or more, a day. It was taking the office staff about two hours a day to dispense medicine. When we decided to dispense prescription medicine only, we offered two specific times during the day to give prescription medicine—11:00 a.m. and 3:00 p.m. A member of the administrative staff dispensed all medicine. This eliminated the possibility of double dosing and other issues. If the prescription called for the medicine to be given twice a day, we would not dispense both doses (since most need to be given 12 hours apart).

We had few exceptions to this rule. One exception was when a child had just received shots. We would dispense Tylenol to that child, at the parent's request, for a couple of days. In the hallway of the center we kept a record of when medicine was dispensed. (A sample Medicine Authorization Form is on page 193 in the Appendix). We also provided two locked spaces for medicine storage (a file box and a small refrigerator).

Key Points to Remember

- Set a medicine policy and stick to it. Make certain it follows licensing standards.
- Provide a medicine sign-in form, locked file box, and small refrigerator to store medicines.
- Assign an office staff member to dispense medicine for the entire center.

For More Information

* For complete bibliography, see pages 209-217.

- This is a basic website for parents and adults regarding medications: http://www.kidneeds.com/diagnostic_categories/articles/med.htm

What to Do When Accidents Occur

The Challenge

I will never forget the day a teacher came running into my office with Christopher bleeding profusely. After I cleaned up the blood, I discovered a cut on his chin that I thought would require stitches.

Solutions

First, I calmed Christopher. Next, I informed Christopher's mother, who happened to be a teacher. She immediately took Christopher to the emergency room, and he received many stitches. We completed a thorough accident report (see Sample Accident/Injury Report on page 194 in the Appendix). One question on the report is, "What were the circumstances surrounding this accident?" In this case, a child pushed Christopher in the bathroom, and he hit his chin on the sink. The teachers and I discussed ways to prevent this type of accident from occurring in the future. In addition, I contacted our state licensing agency in accordance with the law, because Christopher did have to see a medical professional to care for his injury.

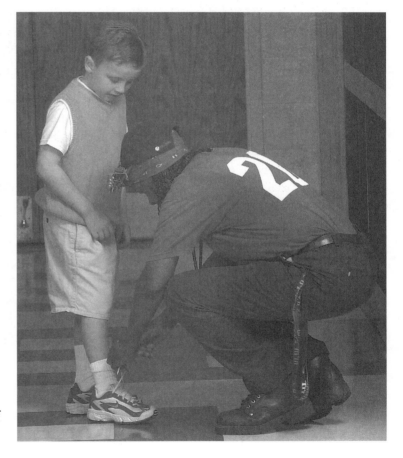

Most accidents that occur do not require a hospital visit and stitches, but they do require our attention. Parents are understandably concerned when they see a "boo boo" or scratch on their child. One of the biggest shocks for parents is the amount of accident reports they receive as their baby becomes a toddler. It is always a good idea to prepare parents for upcoming developmental stages that might offer new challenges for them, as well as their children. Accidents definitely fall into that category. Have a meeting with the parents of the infants. Let them know that exciting changes are happening to their baby—they are growing and moving and with that comes falling. Prepare them for the amount of accidents their toddler may have as they explore their world on two legs instead of "all fours." Inform them of your policy regarding accidents. Let them know that the staff will tell them when their child has an accident and will provide their child with the proper first aid and tender loving care. Convey your commitment to providing a safe environment for children to discover, explore, and experience their environment. Encourage parents to look at this as a positive sign of growth and development whenever possible.

Good communication is the key to keeping accidents from becoming a HUGE issue. Teachers need to be aware of accidents and take the time to write down the events surrounding each instance. Many times, parents asked me about an accident, and I was unable to answer their questions. This led to changes regarding our accident forms:

◆ First, I added an administrative signature on our accident report. The staff was required to get an administrator's signature before informing the parents of the accident. This ensured that someone in the office was aware of every accident in our center and could answer parents' questions regarding the incident.

◆ Second, I had the forms made into duplicates, one for the parent and one for the center. This way I could keep a record in case I ever needed it. This might not be financially feasible for some centers, so you might consider asking the teacher to copy the form, give one to the parents, and then put one in your file box. Or, you could have an accident log sheet for teachers to complete at the end of each day. Another alternative is to ask the parent to sign the report and give it back, making a copy if they request one. Parents' signatures? Yes, by all means! The more information you have on these forms, the better. If anyone ever has a question regarding an accident, a completed form can be very helpful.

What about the mark on the face that has no explanation? Complete an accident report. Be objective and note the time the mark was observed. Make note that the child did not cry or let you know that they had been hurt, but you noticed a mark and proceeded with your policy offering first aid if necessary and completing a report. This should definitely be the exception in a childcare setting and not the norm; however, I am sure most of us have experienced a mysterious injury every now and then.

The bottom line is communication, communication, communication. Parents need information regarding their child's day. When they pick up their child, they rely on us to help fill in the blanks.

Key Points to Remember

◆ Prepare parents for accidents.
◆ Review your accident report and make necessary changes.
◆ Encourage staff to be aware when accidents happen.
◆ Treat the child with TLC or appropriate first aid.
◆ Complete an accident report. Call a parent if necessary.
◆ Notify your licensing agency when a child needs professional medical attention, if required by your state.

For More Information

* For complete bibliography, see pages 209-217.

◆ Check out these sites:
   www.safekids.com
   www.cpsc.gov/cpscpub/pubs/childcare.html
◆ Read this book, *The Perfectly Safe Home* by Jeanne Miller. There is a website, too:
   www.perfectlysafe.com.
◆ Invite a playground inspector out to visit your site. For example, Safeplay Systems can be
   contacted at 1-800-260-7218.
◆ Read "How to Keep Children Safe, Yet Allow Some Risks Necessary for Learning" by
   Amelia Gambetti in the Sep/Oct 2002 issue of *Child Care Information Exchange*.

How to Handle Divorce, Adoption, and Other Challenging Life Events

The Challenge

I have interacted with many varieties of families during my years as an administrator. Single parents, divorced parents, grandparents, and adoptive parents all need care for their young children. I remember one particular scenario: A single mother visited our center, excited about her upcoming adoption of a three-year-old child from Russia. The mother was concerned because her future daughter spoke no English and would not be able to communicate with her. She looked to us for help.

Solutions

Our center was the perfect place for this mother and her new daughter. We had two staff members who had moved to the United States from Russia and were happy to teach the mother some key Russian words and phrases to use on her trip to gather her new daughter and once she returned home. One of the teachers even went to the home of this child when she arrived in the states. These teachers went the extra mile to help this little girl adjust in her new home and her new childcare center. It was only a matter of weeks before this little girl was speaking English to some of her classmates. It was so special to see this child learn and grow in her environment.

I have some personal opinions on this one. I am the mom of three adopted children, and I have encountered several awkward moments over the years. I will never forget the day we visited a new pediatrician's office and the nurse kept asking me, in front of my children, about their "real" mother. I kept insisting I was their "real" mother, and I would be happy to answer any biological information I knew regarding my children. She continued referring to the women who gave birth to my children as the "real" mother. Needless to say, we left that pediatrician's office and never went back. Another time, a child informed my son that he had another mother before me. My son looked at him in horror and turned to me for answers. I stepped in and shared that what that child meant to say was that another lady grew him in her uterus because my uterus cannot grow babies. I assured him that I had always been his mommy. My children look like my husband and me, but some children look totally different than their parents. Be prepared for children to ask, "Why don't I look like my mommy or daddy?" You need to have an answer and help staff members have an answer, too. My suggestion is to be honest, providing only as much information as needed. I refer to the women who gave life to my children as life givers or baby growers. It is not as confusing as "birth mother." I remember the day we were visiting a friend in the hospital and a new mom was being wheeled out with her new baby and her preschooler. My son asked the little boy, "Who grew your new baby for you?" I knew that it was time for a little more information. I shared with John Michael that some women can grow their own babies in their tummies and some cannot. The ones who cannot are very thankful for the women who grow babies for them. My husband and I are very thankful for the life givers of our children.

I understand that there are many family situations that are not this happy. One situation that immediately comes to mind is divorce. On several occasions, parents have asked me to testify in court that they are "wonderful parents." I have always declined. It is not our place to say one parent is better than another. However, it is our place to care for the children during these tough times. We are in the business of childcare, and the children are our first concern. I do provide information for parents to help them work through this time with their child. I keep a file of books, articles, websites, and other material that might be helpful. (For a complete list of helpful resources, see Every Family Is Different on page 195 in the Appendix.) I also suggest that the children talk to a counselor.

All staff should be trained to be on the lookout for behavior changes in children during life-changing events such as divorce, the birth of a new baby, moving, and any other potentially stressful life event. Documenting any changes can be helpful to the teachers and the parents. Children will often act out their feelings instead of sharing them. Offering a troubled child items such as puppets or dolls can help him act out his feelings. If necessary, meet with the parents and, together, create a plan to help the child through this transitional time. Don't hesitate to suggest professional counselors to help out if necessary.

Key Points to Remember

◆ Be sensitive to the needs of individual families. Remember that most families are not made up of mom, dad, two kids, and a dog.

◆ Do not assume anything.

◆ Be aware of behavior changes in children. Offer extra TLC. Document changes for necessary reflection, referrals.

◆ Be careful not to get too involved in adult issues; stay focused on the child.

For More Information

* For complete bibliography, see pages 209-217.

◆ Check out these books for welcoming a new baby in the home:
   Just Like a Baby by Rebecca Bon
   The New Baby by Fred Rogers

◆ These are a few of my favorite adoption books:
   Happy Adoption Day by John McCutcheon
   Tell Me Again About the Night I Was Born by Jamie Lee Curtis

◆ Contact an adoption attorney—I personally recommend Ruth Claiborne and Lori Surmay, 404-521-2100.

◆ Books on divorce include:
   Dinosaurs Divorce Laurence Brown
   Let's Talk About It: Divorce by Fred Rogers

◆ Read the article "Working With Non-Traditional Families" by Lisa Eisenbud in the March/April 2002 *Child Care Information Exchange*.

What to Do When a Child Dies

The Challenge

The center had just closed for the evening, and I was standing in my office talking with the assistant director when the phone rang. It was a parent in our program calling to share the bad news. A child in our program, Michael, was at a park with his mom and a friend when he was hit by a car. It was bad; he was unconscious. The assistant director and I rushed to be with this single mother as she was struggling to deal with the reality of this tragedy. A few days later, Michael died. I can still remember his funeral. He was buried in a casket wearing his favorite pajamas and cowboy boots and surrounded by his favorite toys. It was tragic.

Solutions

This was a tough one. We had to deal with this tragedy on so many levels. First, we offered assistance to the parents of the children in the center as they told their children what had happened. We suggested that they tell the children that, when Michael was hit by a car, it broke his body. The doctors worked and worked, but they could not fix his body. We suggested comparing it to a toy. Sometimes toys, even our favorite toys, break beyond repair. No matter how badly we want these toys fixed, they are not fixable. This is the same with death.

Next, I bought some new puppets, and we used them to talk with the children in Michael's class and other classes that knew him. We allowed the children to use the puppets to talk about Michael's death with each other. We had several children question where Michael's home was now, question their own death, and share their sadness. In addition, because the center was church-based, we celebrated Michael in Heaven. One Saturday after the funeral we invited all of the families to the center for a special "Michael Celebration." We read *The*

Littlest Angel by Charles Tazewell, and the children drew pictures for Michael. We placed the pictures in helium balloons and released them into the sky for Michael. It was a special day.

Finally, we started a resource library in Michael's honor. One of our parents was a skilled craftsman, and he made a beautiful cabinet for the books. We had a large plaque made with Michael's picture on it so everyone could remember his smile. On Michael's birthday, we dedicated the library and invited all of his former classmates to join us and bring a book in Michael's honor.

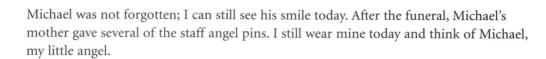

Michael was not forgotten; I can still see his smile today. After the funeral, Michael's mother gave several of the staff angel pins. I still wear mine today and think of Michael, my little angel.

We cannot hide from death. Whether it is a mother with cancer, a stillborn baby, or a pet cat, death will affect the children in our centers, and we need to be prepared. There are many good books on death that you should have in your school library. If you read a good article in an early childhood magazine, save it in a file folder marked "About Death" for future reference.

Key Points to Remember

◆ Be prepared to talk about death with parents and children. I compare dying to a broken toy that cannot be fixed. Someone who is dead has a broken body that could not be fixed. Use this comparison or another one that is meaningful to you and your staff.

◆ Have articles and books on death, especially children's books, in your school library.

◆ Be sensitive and think of opportunities to remember the person or pet that died.

For More Information

* For complete bibliography, see pages 209-217.

◆ Start collecting some of these books for your library:
   Everett Anderson's Goodbye by Lucille Clifton
   The Littlest Angel by Charles Tazewell
   Sad Isn't Sad by Michaelene Mundy
   Sophie by Mem Fox
   The Very Best of Friends by Margaret Wild

◆ Contact a grief counselor in your area and ask for pamphlets, articles, and other information for your resource library.

◆ Visit www.griefcounselors.com. You'll find a good article on their site entitled, "Helping Children Deal with Loss Through the Journaling Process" by Katherine Dorn Zotovich.

◆ "Painting a Tragedy: Young Children Process the Events of September 11" by Toni Gross and Sydney Gurewitz Clemens can be read in the May 2002 issue of *Young Children*. Contact NAEYC at www.naeyc.org for a back issue.

How to Create and Manage Classroom Memories

The Challenge

When you walk into a classroom it is usually full of children's artwork and creations. In a box somewhere the teacher has photographs and more memorabilia items from field trips and special events. Should you throw out these items, pack them in storage, or see just how many will fit into each box?

Solutions

The first thing I did was facilitate a training with the staff on this subject. In the training we discussed memory walls, memory boxes, and memory folders, as well as memory-making environmental changes. Memory walls are made up of photos and children's creations. These areas are decorated in order to display memories that are important to the class. The display should be labeled so parents can recognize the special event. I suggest using the largest wall in your classroom as your memory wall and building on it. (Be sure it is hung at the children's eye level.) It is better to leave pictures up so that children can go back and reflect on the events they have participated in over the year. Start with lots of photographs. Don't limit your picture taking to field trips. Take pictures of children engaging in play, discovering something new, or experiencing their environment. Taking the time to create words to complement the photographs is important, as it completes the story. Fill in with artwork, special memorabilia,

and creations. This will be the favorite wall in your classroom.

Memory boxes are also a great addition to the classroom. Ask each child to bring in a shoebox or other small box that can be decorated. Provide collage materials for the children to personalize their boxes. Set aside a special area in the classroom for the memory boxes. Throughout the year, children will find treasures, make treasures, or bring in treasures that they would like to keep. These are the items that the child puts in his or her memory box. From time to time, children can "share" their memory boxes with the others in the class. At the end of the year, the child can take the memory box home to treasure throughout his or her life.

Memory folders are for the teacher to store memories throughout the year for each child. Each child will need a large folder with his or her name on it. In this folder, keep

some of the child's artwork, special projects, and special memories (and photographs, if possible) you have of that child. Notes and observations about that child can be included in the folder, as well. During end-of-the-year parent conferences, present this folder to the parents as a gift. Parents can transfer the items in the folder into a special book to keep and pass on to their child later in life.

Everyday activities such as baking bread, potting plants, and pulling up the shades will create memories for the children in your center. Think of your own childhood—what memories do you have? Do you remember playing in the mud or learning to tie your shoe? We have the privilege of participating in the memory-making process of many children. Make it your program's priority to provide a place where happy memories can be made.

Key Points to Remember

- ◆ Provide staff training on the subject of making memories.
- ◆ Memory walls, memory boxes, and memory folders are all great tools for capturing memory-making events.
- ◆ Include sensory-associated events in your everyday environment, for example, baking bread, potting plants, and changing the lighting.
- ◆ Remember that children will make memories throughout childhood. Your center is a large part of that memory base.

For More Information

* For complete bibliography, see pages 209-217.

- ◆ Check out the following books:
  My Mama Had a Dancing Heart by Libba Moore Gray
  When I Was Little: A Four-Year-Old's Memoir of Her Youth by Jamie Lee Curtis
  Wilfred Gordon McDonald Partridge by Mem Fox
- ◆ Visit the web site www.turnthepage.com and check out the song "Memories" by Bev Bos and Michael Leeman. You can also call 1-800-959-5549 to order by phone.

Challenges Related to Parents

CHAPTER 3

How to Give Prospective Parents Tours of the Center

The Challenge

Do you ever question your procedure for giving tours? I did. I wanted prospective parents to know that we had an open-door policy, but it seemed as if they were always dropping by at the wrong time. I found that I could not always spend adequate time with them when they dropped in.

Solutions

I met with the assistant director, and together we came up with the following plan:

1. Train other staff members to give tours to parents who drop by. We trained two senior staff members to facilitate tours if we were unavailable.

2. Offer several time options to parents who call to schedule a tour. We decided on 10:00 a.m., 1:00 p.m., or 4:00 p.m. This was to ensure that both office staff members could be present, one to

facilitate the tour and one to cover the office. We kept a tour calendar in the office where we wrote down the day and time of the tour, as well as the person who scheduled the tour and the person who was planning on giving the tour. As the director, I tried to give tours to as many prospective parents as possible. If prospective parents could not visit during one of the above mentioned times, we would try to schedule a tour at their convenience. We always invited prospective parents to stop by and visit the center at any time. However, we let them know that we could not guarantee a tour. This allowed us to keep our open-door policy without feeling as if we were giving drop-in tours all day.

3. Train every staff member on appropriate ways to greet prospective parents during a tour. It is important for the staff member to take a brief moment and acknowledge the visitor in his or her classroom. A kind "hello" or "thanks for stopping in" works fine.

4. Ask parents to complete a visitor card (see Sample Visitor Card on page 196 of the Appendix). This card is used as a resource for the office. File the cards alphabetically and include information such as parent's name, child's name and date of birth, address, phone number (both work and home), and date of visit. There is also a space marked "office only" for the name of the person who gave the tour and any follow-up with the parents. When the child enrolls in the program, place the visitor card in the child's file. It is also a good research tool for marketing purposes.

My motto is that the purpose of a tour is to help educate prospective parents about quality childcare and inform them about the program, NOT to sell them on a particular center. I believe that if parents are well informed about what they believe will be good for their child, they will choose the best center for their family.

Key Points to Remember

- Have plenty of staff members trained to facilitate tours.
- Schedule tours for prospective parents; have specific times for tours.
- Train all staff on greeting prospective parents.
- Ask prospective parents to complete a visitor's card.
- Provide an educational and informative tour as opposed to a persuasive tour.

For More Information

* For complete bibliography, see pages 209-217.

- www.babycare.com provides a sample tour sheet for parents.
- *Preschool for Parents* by Diane Trister Dodge is a good resource for parents looking for a quality program.

How to Handle Offering References to Parents

The Challenge

As a director, parents often asked me for references during a tour. I was never prepared to give them parent names, so I had to tell them I would ask a few parents to call them within a few days. Then I would ask parents whom I knew had positive feelings about our program to call the prospective parents. However, I felt this was cheating parents who were asking for an honest opinion of our center.

Solutions

I decided to ask parents in our program for their opinions. I explained the situation, and I asked the parents for help in two ways:

1. Parents who were willing could write a reference letter that we could show to prospective parents.
2. Parents who were willing could offer their time to prospective parents by adding their name and number to a reference list.

I was pleasantly surprised at the number of reference letters I received. The parents who wrote letters were passionate about the program and usually mentioned specific things they appreciated about the staff and the environment. Most parents included their home and business phone numbers in their letters. I compiled the letters in an attractive notebook and kept it in the office. I also included some photos of our staff and children engaged in play. This gave prospective parents a sense of our program that they might not see if they toured early in the morning or at naptime. I made copies of the reference letters to give to prospective parents upon request. In addition, I included a reference list in our tour package. The tour package also included a letter from me thanking them for touring our center, an

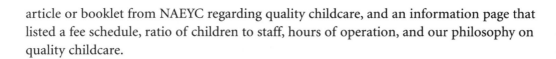

article or booklet from NAEYC regarding quality childcare, and an information page that listed a fee schedule, ratio of children to staff, hours of operation, and our philosophy on quality childcare.

Prospective parents were very pleased to know that so many parents had volunteered to share their opinions and that we had taken the time to organize letters, names, and numbers that would help them in making such an important decision for their child.

Key Points to Remember

- ◆ Ask parents who are willing to write a reference letter for your center.
- ◆ Ask parents who are willing to put their names and phone numbers on a reference list.
- ◆ Compile the reference letters and put them in a notebook.
- ◆ Compile the phone numbers and have them available for prospective parents.

For More Information

* For complete bibliography, see pages 209-217.

- ◆ www.childcaredirectory.com/tips.html is another helpful resource for parents that you might want to include in your reference section.

How to Handle Enrollment

The Challenge

You gave a tour to prospective parents, explained how the center operates, and provided them with the information in the tour package. They have decided to enroll their child in your center. How do you handle the enrollment procedure?

Solutions

Welcoming a family into your program is an important part of creating community in your center. When parents decided to enroll their child, we asked them to come in for a brief visit to the center. We encouraged the parents to bring their child along so the child could see his or her new classroom and the center. During the visit, we provided the parents with a parent handbook (see page 197 in the Appendix for a list of the components) and the necessary paperwork to enroll their child. Before the parents left, we decided on an enrollment process for their child, which included scheduled visits and an official enrollment date. Every enrollment will be different. Some children will need to visit several times, while others may be fine after one visit. The enrollment forms, including all required medical forms, MUST be returned before the child is allowed to enroll. If you collect everything before the child actually attends, there shouldn't be any problems even if the child has an accident the very first day (which hopefully will never happen).

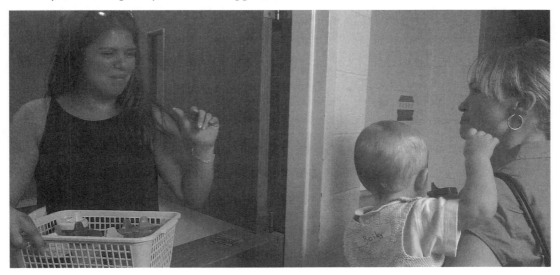

The first day of school should be special for the child and the parent. I always encouraged the teachers to take photographs of the children the first day as a memory for the parents. First-time parents have an especially hard time dropping off their child for the first time. When I dropped off my first child for the first time, I cried for 15 minutes (and I was only headed to work down the hall in the same center!). That experience taught me just how compassionate we need to be in this situation. I headed to a wholesale club and bought lots of the travel-size boxes of tissue. If a parent appeared even a little upset before he or she left, I gave him or her a box of tissues with my business card taped on it. On the business card I wrote, "It is okay to call." This set the tone with new parents and said to them, We care about you as well as your child. It also let them know that it was okay to call to check on their child. To take it a step further, I asked the teachers to take time and call the parents at some point during that first day, assuring them that their child was okay. Finally, I asked a current parent from the child's classroom to call the new family and welcome them to the center.

Key Points to Remember

◆   Encourage parents to visit the program with their child to pick up enrollment papers.

◆   Schedule visits for the new child.

◆   Collect necessary enrollment forms.

◆   Welcome the family on their first day! (Provide tissues if necessary.)

◆   Take pictures of the child engaged in play the first day and offer them to the parents for their memory book.

◆   Ask a parent from the child's new classroom to call and welcome the family to the center.

For More Information

* For complete bibliography, see pages 209-217.

◆ Read the article "Making Families Welcome" in the Sept/Oct 2002 issue of *Child Care Information Exchange.*

◆ The Child Care Group offers "You and Your Baby Start Child Care" and "James and Child Care" as resources to give to parents in preparation for their child's first day. Call 888-8child8 or go online at www.ccgroup.org to place your order.

◆ This website offers a great article to help parents get ready for their child's first day of school. http://www.pueblo.gsa.gov/cic_text/children/firstday/firstday.htm

◆ Read the article "Here, We Call It 'Drop Off and Pick Up'" by Rebecca S. New in the March 1999 issue of *Young Children.*

How to Conduct Parent Orientation

The Challenge

First, you gave tours to prospective parents, and then you helped the parents and children through enrollment. Now it's time for orientation. Do you sometimes feel like it never ends? I often had those feelings myself.

Solutions

Most centers have two types of orientation: first-time orientation and back-to-school orientation. I will address them both.

First-Time Orientation—I believe the best way to handle this is with a one-on-one meeting with the parents during the child's first two weeks of school. The sooner you make a connection with the parents, the fewer headaches you will have when there are issues that you need to address. Meeting with the parents early on lets them know that you are willing to make time for them, and they will be more willing to go straight to you if a problem arises. If several families enroll at one time, I think it is fine to have a small group orientation. (Lunch time might work best for this.) When you schedule the orientation, inform the parents that you will be answering any questions they might have at this point and that you will be asking them to sign a statement saying they have read the parent handbook. This will allow the parents to be better prepared for the meeting and is a nice way to encourage them to actually read the parent handbook.

During the orientation, share your enthusiasm that the parents have chosen to entrust the care of their child(ren) to your staff and your program, and thank them for the opportunity to partner with them on this journey. Highlight important policies and procedures, such as dispensing medicine and sick and late policies. Reiterate your vision for the program (see sample on page 112, Why Having a Vision Is Important) and your philosophy (see sample on page 198 in the Appendix) regarding early childhood education. Even if you tell the parents on many occasions that your staff understands that children learn best through first-hand experiences, many parents may still not understand what this means. Provide examples for them, such as learning language. Describe how your program promotes language and literacy in a hands-on manner. Show them what a lesson plan looks like in your center. Offer appropriate articles, websites, and other resources (see the list of books for a parent resource library in the Appendix on page 191) if they want to read more. Answer any questions the parents might have at this point. Lastly, ask the parents to sign a statement that says they have read the parent handbook. Put this statement in the child's file.

Back-to-School Orientation—This type of orientation only applies if you follow a typical school year and rotate children at a certain time. We moved children once a year (with the exception of infants and toddlers), so we had a back-to-school orientation every fall. I saw this time as an opportunity to help parents learn what went on day to day in our program. Every summer the staff got together to plan orientation. We decided to keep the day the same (Saturday), but change the format slightly every year. We offered two times during the day when parents could attend an orientation session—one in the morning and one in early afternoon. This helped control the group size and allowed the staff to have more one-on-one communication with the parents. We usually began orientation with some type of skit introducing the staff. Parents really enjoyed getting to see and hear the names of the entire staff. Then the staff took the children to another room for a fun activity (babies and young toddlers usually stayed with their parents). This allowed the parents to participate and listen. Next, a staff member (usually the assistant director) would facilitate some type of ice breaker to help the parents get to know each other better (see page 199 in the Appendix for a list of Sample Ice Breakers for Parents and Staff). Following the ice breaker, I shared the goals the staff had set for the year and challenged the parents to set goals for their families as well. Finally, parents were invited to pick up their child from the activity room and visit their child's new classroom for punch and cookies. The teacher welcomed the parents and spent time getting to know everyone. The entire orientation lasted about an hour, and everyone agreed that it was time well spent.

Key Points to Remember

◆ Take time to orient parents.
◆ Involve the staff in the back-to-school orientation.

For More Information

* For complete bibliography, see pages 209-217.

◆ Read *Blueprint for Action: Achieving Center Based Change Through Staff Development* by Paula Jorde Bloom, Marilyn Sheerer, and Joan Britz.

How to Help Parents Get to Know Staff

The Challenge

Some parents have difficulty remembering staff names and faces. Parents also become confused when teachers must move from one class to another from time to time. They feel awkward because they don't know the teacher in their child's classroom.

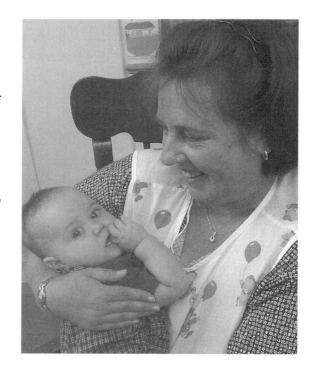

Solutions

To alleviate the confusion, I went on a mission. I used the school camera to take pictures of every staff member in our program. I also asked the staff to complete a short questionnaire similar to the following:

Name _____

Early childhood background _____
_____

Favorite childhood memory _____
_____
_____

When I go home at the end of the day, I like to _____
_____

Family information _____

I gathered the information and wrote a short paragraph describing each staff member. I bought plastic frames for each staff member to decorate, and I placed their picture and the short paragraphs inside. We hung the frames outside the classroom doors for parents and guests to see. Parents thanked us, and all of the decorated frames made our halls look festive.

In addition, I invited the staff members to write articles for the monthly newsletter. The only requirement was that the topic needed to mean something to the author. The topics included things such as gardening, childhood stories, favorite recipes, and activities for home. My initial reason for doing this was to provide parents with a way of getting to know some of the other teachers. The amazing thing was how the teachers responded to this request. I believe it really gave them an opportunity to express themselves in a different way. Give it a try! Not only will it help teachers and parents, it will also help you. If you are like me, your newsletter always ends up with an empty space that needs to be filled. This is a great way to fill that space!

Key Points to Remember

- ◆ Ask staff members to complete a questionnaire.
- ◆ Write a short paragraph about each staff member.
- ◆ Take pictures of staff.
- ◆ Put pictures and short paragraphs in frames.
- ◆ Hang outside the appropriate classroom.
- ◆ Invite teachers to contribute articles to the monthly newsletter.
- ◆ Enjoy having someone help you with the newsletter.

For More Information

* For complete bibliography, see pages 209-217.

- ◆ Read *Training Teachers* by Margie Carter and Deb Curtis.

How to Encourage Parent Involvement

The Challenge

One of the most basic, universal questions directors ask is, "How do I get parents involved in my program?"

Solutions

The first question to ask yourself is why you want parents involved in your program. The *most important* reason is to involve them in their child's life experiences. Of course, there will be occasions when you need their help and they will be helpful, but the primary reason is for the children. If you approach this issue from the child's perspective, it will help make soliciting parents easier. So, how do you get them involved? A few suggestions are:

◆ Invite parents to come in and read to the children.
◆ Have one parent each week participate in show and tell. Encourage the parent to bring a favorite childhood item to share with the class.
◆ Invite parents to participate in field trips and special events.
◆ Ask parents to share their culture and heritage with the class by helping with cooking projects or bringing in special artifacts or clothing.

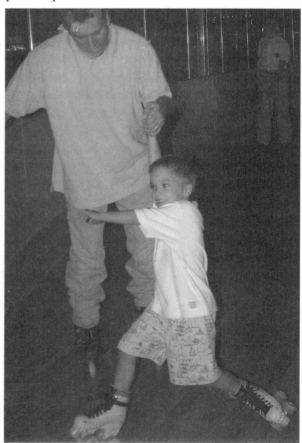

At my last center, I was very fortunate because I had a group of parents who thrived on involvement. A few parents talked to each other, and then asked me if we could start parent committees. I suggested that we survey all the parents and see if there was an interest (see Sample Parent Involvement Survey on page 201 in the Appendix). One of the parents offered to create and oversee the survey process, and I gratefully accepted! The surveys came back with positive responses; many parents were interested and willing to serve on a committee.

I met with the few parents who initiated this idea, and we created the following committees:

- Teacher Appreciation
- Special Events
- Facility and Grounds
- Welcoming
- Memory
- Fellowship

I am not kidding when I say this was all the parents' idea. This group of parents presented the list of committees with a short job description for each and solicited volunteers one morning in the hallway of the center, offering doughnuts and coffee to all who stopped by. It was a huge success. Most parents volunteered and handled all of it. The only thing I asked of the committee chairs was to keep me informed and allow me to have a final vote in decisions. Only once did I veto something that a committee really wanted. I did not feel it was in the best interest of the center. The committee wanted to ask parents to volunteer in the center for an entire day so the staff could attend the NAEYC conference together. It was being held in our city that year, and they thought we might enjoy attending together. I said thanks, but no thanks. However, we did have several parents volunteer that week so a few staff members could attend the conference each day. I believe the real reason the parents were so involved was because of a few passionate women. These women had a vision, and they pursued it. They were *fire starters**, and our entire center benefited. Be on the lookout for passionate parents in your program and encourage them to be fire starters, too.

Fire starters are people whose enthusiasm and passion burn in them and they create "fires" with their flaming passions wherever they go.

Key Points to Remember

- Ask yourself why you want parents involved.
- Read and try the above tips.
- Thank parents for their involvement.

For More Information

* For complete bibliography, see pages 209-217.

- Read the article "From Borders to Bridges: Transforming Our Relationships With Parents" by Ann Pelo in the Sept/Oct 2002 of *Child Care Information Exchange*.
- Read the following articles in the November 2000 issue of *Young Children*:
    "Parent Involvement in the Classroom" by Nancy DeSteno
    "Planning Family Involvement in Early Childhood Programs" by Judith Kieff and Karyn Wellhousen.

How to Create a Sense of Community

The Challenge

The children in your center spend many hours in your care each day. In fact, many children spend the majority of their waking hours with you and your staff. This may lead you to question, "Are we just a childcare center?"

Solutions

When we care for children, we are caring for their entire family. Our work allows parents to go to work each day with the peace of mind that their child is safe. We are there for the children when they begin to walk, talk, and write their names. Ours is a business of families, and because there are many families in our business, I like to look at it as its own community. How do we nurture our community? There are many answers, such as:

◆   Picnics at a local park—We usually held these twice a year; one was theme-related and one was not. Families can bring the meal for their own family, the center can provide the meal at a cost to the parents, or parents can each bring something to share. Modify this idea if necessary, and have fun!

◆   Thanksgiving dinner—This was one of my favorite events. The location of your center and room space will determine how you structure this event. If your program is part of a larger facility, you can have the entire center share this meal. This is what my center did and it was amazing. The school provided the meat and the parents brought the side dishes. The children even contributed a dish, usually a salad. One year we had over 400 people attend this event (including the children, of course). Even if you don't have the space to seat 400 people, you can still enjoy this meal together in the individual classrooms. You will have to think about getting extra chairs or providing areas to sit on the floor. We also encouraged participants to share what they were thankful for that year.

◆   Special breakfasts—Our center did not serve breakfast on a regular basis so this was always a treat. Around Mother's Day, we always planned "Muffins with Mom." We encouraged the mothers to drop off their children a little early that morning in order to share breakfast with their child. The children made placemats for their moms, and they enjoyed a nice breakfast together. Children who did not have mothers or whose mothers were unable to attend were encouraged to bring along another special person, male or female. Around Father's Day, we had "Donuts with Dad" and handled it in a similar way. One other time during the year, we hosted "Bring a Parent for Breakfast Day." Each staff member brought a breakfast dish to share as a way to thank the parents for all they had done for the staff and the center. All of these events were well received.

◆   Family portraits—Have a professional photographer come to your center to take family portraits.

◆ Open-door policy—To encourage parent involvement, have an open-door policy for parents to visit the center any time throughout the day. For example, depending on the location of your center, you may or may not have lunch-time visitors. Because our center was located close to work for many families, we had many visitors, especially parents of infants. Many of the nursing mothers would come over on their lunch break and offer a feeding to their baby. We were fortunate to have a private place for them to go if they desired. If you don't have a separate area, try and provide an area of the room away from the door and windows to offer a little privacy. A few of the parents of preschoolers would have lunch with their children on a regular basis. Most parents of toddlers did not come by very often because it is hard for toddlers to understand that their parent is only visiting and will leave soon.

Key Points to Remember

◆ Recognize that you are more than just a childcare center.
◆ Provide opportunities for nurturing the family.
◆ Survey parents for new ideas (see Sample Community Survey on page 202 of the Appendix).

For More Information

* For complete bibliography, see pages 209-217.

◆ Read *Making a Difference: A Parent's Guide to Advocacy and Community Action* by Diane Charnov and Carolyn Rutsch.

How to Deal With the Overwhelmed Parent

The Challenge

How many times have you greeted a parent at the door only to find him or her exhausted and overwhelmed?

Solutions

I did not originally include this subject in the book. Nancy Alexander, author of *Early Childhood Workshops that Work* and a former center director, brought it to my attention, and I am thankful she did. After discussing this issue with Nancy, I remembered having parents who were definitely on edge. Often, these parents would drop off their children when the doors opened and pick them up right before closing time. These parents were so tired that they did not have time to listen to news about their child's day. Sometimes they even cancelled their parent conference.

What is a director to do? I believe this is when you make time to talk with the parent. For example, when the parent drops off his or her child, invite him or her for coffee. Be persistent. It might take several tries or a different approach before the parent responds. When you finally do meet with the parent, share your support and concerns. Encourage the parent to take a break, or to talk to a friend or a counselor. Explain that you are concerned for the child because you sense that the parent is exhausted at the end of the day. Offer any help you or your program feels comfortable giving. Maybe the parent is dealing with the death or serious illness of a family member or close friend, having a conflict with his or her spouse, or experiencing problems at work. Who knows? What you do know is that all children need an attentive parent, someone who can take time at the end of a day to listen to what his or her children have to say about their experiences that day. These parents may already feel guilty, and we do not need to add to their guilt. Simply try to guide them to evaluate their lives, get any help they need, and encourage and support them on their journey.

Key Points to Remember

◆ Many parents are overwhelmed with everyday life.
◆ Invite the parent in for some coffee and a heart-to-heart chat.
◆ Offer any help or resources you have available.
◆ Listen, and then encourage and support their plans.

For More Information

* For complete bibliography, see pages 209-217.

◆ Add *The Busy Mom* by Sharon Murphy Yates to your resource library.
◆ Look up the following websites:
    www.npin.org/library/2001/n00564/2.html has several articles on this topic.
    www.theparentclub.com is where many parents go to find support.
    www.familyeducation.com has some great stress-relief tips for busy parents.

How to Provide Resources for Parents

The Challenge

A parent says, "I think my 18-month-old is ready to potty train. She really likes to sit on the potty and she can say 'pee-pee.'" Does this sound familiar? Or, how about, "Why is my child being bitten in his toddler classroom? There must be something wrong with the child who is biting my son." What is the best way to respond to sensitive questions such as these?

Solutions

I think the best way to address and educate parents about sensitive issues is before the issues arise. Toddlers seem to experience the most changes in the shortest amount of time. To help parents better understand what was ahead, I hosted a meeting for the parents of infants in my program. This way, we could begin to prepare parents for what they and their children would be experiencing over the next couple of years. I informed the parents of all the exciting

things they had to look forward to in the toddler years, such as walking, talking, potty training, and many other important milestones. I also informed them of the developmental stages that occur as children move from dependent infant to independent toddler. For example, after toddlers get their teeth, they may begin to bite other children. I shared our policy on biting and offered articles on the subject. Talking and sharing information with the parents before the first bite helps them understand the developmental side of biting before their emotions get involved. This is the same with potty training, sharing, and other behavior issues.

I found these meetings well worth the time. They are another example of looking at your program as a community. In addition, first-time parents appreciate having the opportunity to ask the staff and more experienced parents questions regarding the upcoming stage.

Consider having this type of meeting for parents of older toddlers to cover the preschool years. For example, I remember when we decided to switch from having separate classrooms for three-, four-, and five-year-olds to multi-age classrooms. We had several parent meetings to discuss the new classrooms and how it would benefit the children.

If a parent joins your program after you have had this meeting or before you have begun these meetings, don't worry. My suggestion is simply to ask the parent a few questions regarding his or her child. Here's an example. The mother of 18-month-old Caroline approaches you and says that she thinks her child is ready for potty training. Ask her some questions, such as: "Is Caroline able to take off and put on her own clothes? Does she stay dry for long periods of time? Does she tell you when her diaper is wet or soiled? Can she get on and off the toilet by herself?" Explain to Caroline's mother that these are some signs of readiness, and it sounds as if Caroline is not quite ready. Reassure her that most children are toilet trained by the time they are three and encourage her to keep watching for these signs. Feel free to encourage the parent to talk to the pediatrician at Caroline's next checkup.

Of course, there will also be times when parents approach you about subjects that are unique to their child, such as wetting the bed or having temper tantrums in a store. It's a good idea to keep a file of resource articles that address the many issues children face in the early years. Keep several copies in the file and create a master notebook of the articles. This will prevent you from handing out your last copy and then realize you threw away the journal or magazine. Always get permission before copying copyrighted material. I also think it is a good idea to have a library of child development books and videos that parents can check out. Remember, the more common understanding parents and teachers have, the easier it will be for everyone.

Key Points to Remember

- Try to address issues before they arise.
- Host parent meetings that focus on a specific age to discuss the next stage of development. Supply additional resources such as articles and websites.
- Keep a file of articles on child-related subjects.
- Have a library of books and videos available for parents to check out. (See Essential Books for Parent Library on page 191 in the Appendix for a complete list of resources.)

For More Information

* For complete bibliography, see pages 209-217.

- The *Child Care Information Exchange* now offers Parent Exchange. Look it up on the website: www.childcareexchange.com.
- Teaching Strategies offers a number of resources for parents. Contact the company at www.teachingstrategies.com or 800-637-3652.
- NAEYC offers brochures on a variety of child-related subjects. Check out its website at www.naeyc.org or call 800-424-2460.
- http://misterrogers.org/early_care/using_mrn_fc_pamphlets.asp provides pamphlets for parents.

How to Accommodate (or Not) Special Requests From Parents

The Challenge

One of the most interesting conversations I had when I was a director was with a parent who felt that her 18-month-old was being held back in his toddler classroom. She explained that her son was "advanced" for his age and needed to be challenged. Therefore, she continued, she wanted her son moved up into a two-year-old room. One of the challenges you face as a director is how to accommodate special requests or turn down unreasonable requests from parents.

Solutions

I struggled for the right way to respond to the parent's request. I concluded that this little boy was in the appropriate classroom. There were several children who were due to move up to a two-year-old room before this child, and I could not overlook them just to please this parent. Another question I considered was, "Can an 18-month-old be held back by his peers?" I explained to the parent that this was not something I could do. I wish I could tell you that the parent understood and it worked out okay, but I cannot. The parent, who had been very active in our center and was well-liked by the staff, pulled her child out and moved him into a program where he would be allowed to be in an older class. We were sad to lose that family, but we knew that we could not be everything to everybody.

There are many times when we can and will accommodate a parent's special request. I remember we had a younger sibling going through a separation stage from her parents. The parents asked if they could leave the younger sibling with the older child at drop-off time. We did have to adjust a few things, such as making sure the room was free of toys that were a potential choking hazard and making sure that teacher-children ratios for the younger child's age were being met. Both of those adjustments were manageable for a short time. After about 15 minutes, the younger sibling was ready to go to her own room and it was an easy transition.

The requests parents make vary as much as the children themselves, so there is not a magic answer for how to handle special requests. However, there are a few questions I always asked myself when considering a request:

- ◆ Why is this request being made?
- ◆ Is this a reasonable request?
- ◆ Is it in the best interest of the child involved?
- ◆ Do we have to make any changes that involve money?
- ◆ If so, where will the money come from?
- ◆ How does the staff feel about the request?
- ◆ Will other families be affected? How?
- ◆ Are there any other solutions available?

These questions helped me look at each request individually and objectively. I wanted to help make things easier for parents and I wanted to keep them happy. However, I was not willing to do either at the expense of the child. In the original scenario I mentioned, would it have hurt the child to be in a classroom with older children? Of course not. But, was it in the best

interest of the child? No. Was I willing to lose this family over the situation? I did not think that would happen, but unfortunately, it did. However, I am confident many years later that I acted in the best interests of the child, and that I handled the situation appropriately.

Key Points to Remember

◆   Listen to the parents.
◆   Evaluate their concern or comment, asking yourself the questions on page 98.
◆   Make a decision based on the best interests of the child and the center.

For More Information

* For complete bibliography, see pages 209-217.

◆   Read the article "Empowering Parents?" by Jim Greenman in the March/April 2001 issue of *Child Care Information Exchange*.

How to Conduct Effective Parent Conferences

The Challenge

Conducting effective conferences with parents can be quite challenging. There are many questions about holding parent conferences. What is the purpose of parent conferences? Who should be there? Where should they be held? How long should they last? What should we talk about?

Solutions

What is the purpose? Conferences are an important time in the life of any center. Staff members should look at parents as partners in their program. Encourage staff to consider conferences as a partners' meeting.

Who should be there? Both teachers should be present, along with both parents (if applicable).

Where should they be held? I believe the environment should be comfortable and inviting.

Try to arrange the furniture so you are sitting in a circle instead of across from each other at a table. This will set the tone for the meeting. A circle lets the parents know that you are all in this together instead of the "teachers versus the parents." It adds a nice touch to offer punch and cookies to the parents when they arrive.

How long should they last? At least 30-45 minutes—anything less than that will not allow enough time for any discussion. Try to allow 10 minutes between conferences to cover late arrivals and lengthy discussions.

What should we talk about? Of course, this is the most important element to a successful conference. Start the conference on a positive note; for example, share some of the child's latest art processes. It is nice to provide some samples of the child's work that shows developmental progress. Continue talking about the child's developmental accomplishments. Ask parents to confirm developmental milestones, such as "Does your child point out specific colors when he or she is at home?" If there are issues that need to be addressed, do so at this point. Ask the parents for their input on these issues and, if necessary, work together to develop a plan. (I am talking about minor issues that might occur, such as children not wanting to go outside or saying they are scared at nap time.)

Any serious issues or concerns should be addressed in a separate meeting with the director and not in a parent conference. Offer a few minutes for parents to ask questions about their child's experience in the classroom. If the parents seem reluctant to ask questions or express their feelings regarding their child's care, try asking some of these open-ended questions:

1. How would you say your child has changed since our last meeting?
2. What is your favorite part of your child's stage of development?
3. What, if anything, would you like to see us do differently in your child's classroom?

End the meeting with a few goals you hope to see their child accomplish before the next parent conference and add a positive note about the child. For example, "Your son Jackson is a very good block builder. His constructions are complex, and he builds cooperatively with other children." I suggest going a step further and providing a few photographs that capture their child engaging in the mentioned activity. Remind the parents that you consider them partners and that you are willing to schedule a meeting with them anytime throughout the year.

Key Points to Remember

◆ Make a plan before meeting with parents.
◆ Both teachers should be present.
◆ Create an inviting environment.
◆ Try to spend 30-45 minutes with each family.
◆ Begin and end the conference on a positive note.
◆ Address any minor issues that parents have.
◆ Allow parents the opportunity to address issues.
◆ If necessary, make a plan for the child.
◆ Provide sample artwork and photographs for parents to take home.

For More Information

* For complete bibliography, see pages 209-217.

◆ Read *Focused Portfolios: A Complete Assessment for the Young Child* by Gaye Gronlund and Bev Engel, and *The Portfolio Book: A Step-By-Step Guide for Teachers* by Cathy Grace and Elizabeth Shores.

◆ Consider using *The Creative Curriculum Developmental Continuum Assessment Tool Kit* by Teaching Strategies. More information can be found at www.teachingstrategies.com.

What to Do When Parents Get Angry

The Challenge

Some parents believe anything that goes wrong is the director's fault. Whether it is children biting each other, the toilet breaking, or staff members calling in sick, they feel that it is all your fault. When I was a director, I had parents who got upset and blamed me for almost every subject imaginable. Dealing with angry parents is especially challenging.

Solutions

Most of the time interacting with parents was one my favorite parts of being a director. However, whenever I saw an angry parent headed for my office, I sometimes wished I was invisible. Many times when a parent enters your office, you do not know if the parent will be enjoyable or challenging. You must be ready for both.

In our business we are not taking care of merchandise, we are entrusted with something extremely precious—children. If you remember to look at every situation through the eyes of the parent, it will help your attitude. I remember a particular couple who was furious with me because their son continued to be bitten by the same child. They insisted that the biter had "issues" and that their son was perfect. They even got into an altercation with the parents of the biter. It was a stressful situation that continued for almost a year. Believe it or not, both families did get through the situation and remained at the center until time for kindergarten. Although there were some days when I did not think any of us would make it, we did. I believe the reason we all made it through was the amount of time we spent communicating about the subject.

The following steps outline the process I used to handle this particular issue:

1. I met with the teachers in the classroom to fully understand the situation, and I asked them to keep a journal of the circumstances surrounding the biting incidents.

2. I met with the parents of the victim and the biter separately. I shared with both of them my concern regarding the situation and the steps I planned to take to stop the biting. I reassured the parents of the victim that we did not approve of biting, and that it was a developmental issue that would eventually end. I assured the parents of the biter that they were not to blame and that their child was not biting as a result of something they failed to do. The mother of the biter struggled with guilt surrounding this issue.

3. After one week of observing and journaling, the teachers concluded that the biter tended to bite the victim after the victim pushed or shoved the biter. We decided to add a third teacher in the room to shadow these two children, especially the victim. The reason we asked her to focus on the victim was because if the victim did not push, the biter did not bite. It was rare that the biter would bite another child other than this specific one. The bites dramatically decreased.

4. I asked the teachers to inform me immediately when a bite occurred. After each biting incident, I called the parents of the victim and informed them of the bite. I felt that calling them would be better than telling them during pick-up time when they might be more emotional. I also did the calling instead of asking the teachers to do so. This situation was stressful enough for them, and I thought I could ease some of that by being the one to take the "heat" on the phone.

5. I worked hard on my relationship with both sets of parents. They were angry and frustrated, but I believe they hung in there with me because they knew I was taking steps to solve the problem. I felt I was on the offensive in this situation, which worked to my advantage.

6. The biting did stop and the children remained friends.

This was an extreme situation. It is much easier when a parent is angry over a one-time issue, such as the toilet breaking. Usually, in a situation like this, the parent isn't even angry about the toilet. It's likely that something stressful happened at work or home and when the toilet does not flush, he or she blows up. Don't let those situations get the best of you! Thank them for bringing it to your attention, and then handle the situation. Once it has been taken care of, make a phone call or tell them in person how the situation was solved. Many times the parent will apologize for being angry and that is great. If they do not apologize, just smile and know that you handled yourself professionally.

Key Points to Remember

◆ Take parents' concerns seriously.
◆ Work with staff and make a plan to address their concern.
◆ Keep parents informed of your progress.
◆ Remember, this too shall pass.

For More Information

* For complete bibliography, see pages 209-217.

◆ Read the article "How to Deal with Difficult Parents" by Steve Bro in the April 2001 issue of *Child Care Business.*

◆ "The Bad News Blues: When Messages Aren't Easy to Deliver" by Jane Harris is a great article. Get the back issue of *Child Care Information Exchange,* Sep/Oct 1994, or look it up on www.childcareexchange.com.

◆ The book *Places for Childhoods: Making Quality Happen in the Real World* by Jim Greenman addresses the issue of biting with reprints of two fabulous articles from *Child Care Exchange.* These were the articles I provided for families dealing with biting.

◆ Another good article to read is "Understanding and Preventing Toddler Biting" by Veronica Garcia in the Summer 1999 issue of *Texas Child Care.* Call 512-441-6633 for back issues.

How to Handle Late Pick-Ups

The Challenge

What do you do if a parent disregards one of your policies? When I was a director, I had a parent who ignored our late pick-up policy. The parent was late to pick up his daughter twice one week. I did not charge him a late fee the first time, but the second time I added the charge to his account. The problem was that he refused to pay the late fee and he continued to be late about once a week.

Solutions

This event caused me to re-evaluate our entire late pick-up policy, which was to charge parents a flat fee of $5.00 if they were late. And, we were often late about enforcing the policy. After the incident mentioned above, I decided to make a new late pick-up policy:

◆ $10.00 charge for the first 5 minutes late, and $1.00 for every minute afterwards.

◆ Parents had to pay the fee directly to the staff member who stayed late with the child.

◆ After 3 late pick-ups, the parents received a warning.

◆ After 5 late pick-ups, the parents could be asked to pull their child out of the program.

◆ If the late fee was not paid within one week, we added it to the parents' account and handled it as any other debt.

Creating the new policy was not the hard part; enforcing it was. However, it was much easier for me to demand money for the staff member than for the center. It was hard for any parent to look at their child's teacher and refuse to pay the late fee. As the director, I felt it was important to stay with the teacher and help reinforce our policy with the late parent. It also helped the teacher feel better, knowing she was not going to have to face the parents alone.

The parents' excuses were always good. We heard things from "my meeting was longer than expected" to "the traffic was uncontrollable" to "I lost track of time." Therefore, we decided that the excuse did not matter. We wanted to be there for the parents and to provide a community atmosphere, but we closed at 6:30. Therefore, children needed to be picked up by 6:30—not 6:36. Once we began enforcing our "no-tolerance" policy, the late pick-ups dwindled except for once-in-a-while emergencies. It reduced the stress of the teachers who were responsible for closing each night and who were ready to go home, as well as the children who had been in care all day and did not want to be the last ones there every night.

I know this policy is not warm and fuzzy and might not be popular, but your approach to it can help. Take the offensive approach on this one. Go over your policy with prospective parents, and let them know your reasons for such a tough policy. My reasons were the children and the staff, who were ready to go home at 6:30. I needed parents to respect that. I found that my positive attitude and up-front approach to this subject went a long way.

Key Points to Remember

◆ Review and revise your late pick-up policy, if necessary.
◆ Enforce your policy consistently.

For More Information

* For complete bibliography, see pages 209-217.

◆ This article has some good tips on parent communication, including late pick-up:
   http://ohioline.osu.edu/hyg-fact/5000/5205.html
◆ This article is a good resource for parents:
   http://familyfun.go.com/raisingkids/child/skills/feature/dony87prcaregiver/
◆ Check out this website for more information on creating policies for your program:
   http://www.redleafinstitute.org/Index.cfm?section=BL&Page=BL10

How to Handle Late Drop-Offs

The Challenge

The office phone rang at about 11:00 a.m. and it was Tyler's mom. She was calling to request that lunch be saved for Tyler because she would be dropping him off at noon. This was the second time this had happened in the past couple of weeks, and the teachers were frustrated because this child was disruptive when he arrived and was not ready to take a nap with the rest of the group.

Solutions

When I was a director, our parent handbook stated that our center hours were from 7:00 a.m. – 6:30 p.m. It also suggested that children arrive by 9:30 a.m. in order to get the most from the experiences offered in the classroom. However, in the above situation, Tyler's mother had been traveling and wanted to spend some mornings with her son. I understand that late drop-offs can be a little disruptive to the classroom, but I think a little planning and lots of communication go a long way. My feeling is that we are in the business of supporting families; therefore, forcing a child to come to school instead of spending time with his or her family seems wrong. My solution was to ask the parents to call by 9:00 a.m. if their child was going to attend school late that day so the teachers would have enough time to prepare for lunch and ratio planning. At that point, the teachers could also begin working on a plan for the child's late arrival. If the child is to arrive after lunch, I feel it is okay to ask the parent to feed the child before he or she arrives at school. If the child arrives during nap but will not nap, he or she can participate in some of the activities from that morning. Suggest that the teacher cozy up with the child and read a book, or let the child listen to a book on tape with earphones, play with puzzles, or create a masterpiece with art materials.

Where do you draw the line? I think every family and every situation is different. As long as you and your staff can work out a solution for the late arrival, I suggest you do it. If it exceeds what you and the staff can handle, explain this to the parent and see if you can work out a solution together. Remember, the parents are our partners in this journey and we are all in this for the children. What is truly best for the child? Most of the time when we think things can't work out, it is because it is best for the adults. I encourage you to keep your focus on the child, and most situations will be easier.

Key Points to Remember

- Talk with the parents to find out why the child needs to be dropped off late.
- Talk with the staff and ask them to consider the child's point of view.
- Flexibility is key.

For More Information

* For complete bibliography, see pages 209-217.

◆ The article "The Ten P's of Parent Communication" by Timothy Wayne Borruel is a great resource for your staff. Check it out in the January 2002 issue of *Child Care Information Exchange*.

◆ Read the article "Preparing Parents for Change" by Julie Powers in the September 2001 issue of *Child Care Information Exchange*. This article highlights the importance of communication in a quality early childhood program.

How to Deal With the Academically Minded Parent

The Challenge

While giving tours to parents, I almost expected them to tell me how advanced their child was and how their child needed to be challenged. I was never surprised to hear parents say, "I think my two-year-old is ready to start reading because she knows her ABC's and she loves books."

Solutions

My favorite saying about education is "Educating children begins with educating the adults in their lives." An "advanced" child may be developing at a faster rate in one of the developmental areas, but not in others. For example, the parents of this two-year-old have probably noticed that their child has good verbal skills and has memorized the ABC song. However, this does not mean she has the necessary cognitive or emotional development necessary for reading.

This is when your role as the director is to educate parents about child development and developmentally appropriate practices. The more parents truly understand about what goes on in your center, the easier your job will be in the end. Reassure the parents that your curriculum is based on each individual child, and that your staff is aware of their child's development and will adjust their curriculum accordingly. Sometimes, it helps parents to better understand what their child's day is like by experiencing it themselves.

That is why the staff and I started Parents' Night Out, described below:

1. Start the evening with an ice breaker (see page 199 in the Appendix for a list of Sample Ice Breakers).
2. Have an adult version of circle time. Welcome the parents and invite them to take off their "parent hats" for the night and reach back into childhood. Encourage them to enjoy themselves, meet someone new, and ask questions during the evening. Next, teach the parents a new song and sing one that they might remember from their own childhood. Read an interesting children's book, role modeling as you read.
3. Set up several classrooms with developmentally appropriate art and sensory activities. Have extra teachers on hand to help facilitate the activities.
4. Invite parents to participate in as many activities as possible for about an hour. It is amazing to watch parents forget their responsibilities as grown-ups and remember how to "play" like young children.
5. Serve as a facilitator by moving around the rooms and encouraging play.
6. Take photographs. They look great on a memory wall or in a photo album.
7. Provide a handout that explains each activity and its learning value. Also provide additional resources, such as a listing of books, magazines, websites (see Sample Child Development Handout for Parents' Night Out on page 203 of the Appendix) for parents to research more about child development.

This evening provided parents with a first-hand look at our child-centered philosophy. (We even had moms and dads in their business clothes produce beautiful artwork by tongue painting. It was great!) Keeping the night a mystery contributes to the success. Do not tell parents what will happen or what to wear. It is a great way to help them understand why "play clothes" are so important!

Before we developed Parents' Night Out, I offered educational parent meetings and hardly any parents would show up. When we were planning our first Parents' Night Out, I was not sure what to expect, but I knew I wanted as many parents to attend this evening as possible. The staff had a contest to see which class would have the largest percentage of parents present. The children told the parents about it every day, and we handed out flyers, made banners, offered childcare, and tried to market the night so that everyone wanted to attend. Guess what? Seventy percent of the families were represented that night! That first Parents' Night Out changed our center.

After that evening, I rarely had parents asking when their child would read. They understood that we were preparing their children for reading when they painted, played in dramatic play or with blocks, sculpted playdough, or looked through books. Parents rarely asked a teacher what their child learned that day, because it was evident when they saw the towers built, the artwork displayed, and the seeds growing by the window. They "got it." In fact, one parent moved away and called me for help. After touring several beautiful and expensive centers, she saw no evidence of learning in the centers. She shared that she knew "too much" as a result of being a part of our program and Parents' Night Out.

The next year I did not plan a Parents' Night Out because we did not have many new families, and I thought it would be repetitive. That was a mistake. Many parents asked, "When do we get to play again?" With the help of the staff, we created a second version called Another Parents' Night Out. The format for this evening is as follows:

1. Make the focus of the night imagination. Begin the evening with the staff performing a skit that they wrote. They invite different parents to join them throughout the skit. This sets the tone for an imaginative evening.
2. Direct parents to a room full of costumes and props. Once the parents choose their costumes for the evening, hand them a piece of paper with their identity written on it.
3. Provide dinner for the parents, but they must stay in character. It is such a great time for parents to remember the power of imagination.
4. At the end of dinner, separate the parents into groups and ask them to make up a commercial using a bag of materials provided for them. Capture the evening with video and photos.
5. Ask participants to stop by the story room where colored pencils, crayons, and markers are on the tables. Encourage the parents to tell their story by drawing a picture or writing in the journals provided. Later, use the pictures and writings to create memory books for the children and the center.
6. Again, information is provided to share the importance of dramatic play in the life of a young child.

Both evenings were a huge success. From that point on, we offered a Parents' Night Out every year. Many of our parents went from wanting their child to read by the age of three to becoming true advocates of "real" appropriate learning.

Key Points to Remember

◆ Once again, listen to the parents.
◆ Educate, educate, educate (the parents) on child development.
◆ Consider a Parents' Night Out to help parents experience child development.
◆ Inform parents of the activities and experiences that their children are receiving.
◆ Reassure the parents that you will change the curriculum as necessary to meet the needs of their child.

For More Information

* For complete bibliography, see pages 209-217.

- Go to www.teachingstrategies.com and read "ABC's and 123's," an excerpt from the *Parent's Guide to Early Childhood Programs* by Teaching Strategies.
- Put the following book in the parent resource library: *The Trouble With Perfect: How Parents Avoid the Over Achievement Trap and Still Raise Successful Children* by Elisabeth Guthrie and Kathy Matthews.
- Also include the classic book, *The Hurried Child* by David Elkind.

How to Create Memories for Parents

The Challenge

As the director, I wanted parents and children to participate in memory-making moments.

Solutions

I invited parents to reminisce about their own childhoods and asked them to share their memories with us. We did this in several ways:

- We asked parents to come into the classroom and share their childhood memories.
- If parents had home movies, we asked them to share those with us.
- We asked parents to write down a story from their childhood, including pictures when possible.
- We invited parents to bring in any of their favorite childhood toys and share them with their child's class.

We wanted everyone to enjoy these childhood stories, so we asked parents if we could share some of their memories in our monthly newsletter. If possible, we included a childhood photo along with the story. The stories were enjoyed by all and helped us get to know the parents in a different light.

Next, I wanted to provide a way to help children remember their parents while they were separated for the day. We did this in the four ways listed on the next page:

1. We asked parents to provide current photographs of their family, and we made family books that we kept in the book center.
2. We asked parents to create special notes that children could keep in their cubbies or memory boxes.
3. We asked parents to record a message to their child and we kept the tape in the listening center.
4. We asked parents to record themselves reading one of their child's favorite books. (You can let parents borrow a tape recorder overnight or use it in the center after drop-off or pick-up time.) We kept the book and tape in the listening center for the child to enjoy.

Key Points to Remember

◆ Encourage parents to think about their own childhoods.
◆ Invite parents to participate in your program by sharing some of their childhood memories.
◆ Encourage parents to take time to provide memories of themselves for their children to have at school.

For More Information

* For complete bibliography, see pages 209-217.

◆ There are lots of websites about making memories:
www.familyfun.go.com/crafts/cutpaste/feature/char38scraps/char38scraps.html
www.familyinternet.about.com/library/weekly
www.creativehomemaking.com/articles/092402a.shtml

Challenges Related to the Details of Directing a Center

CHAPTER 4

Why Having a Vision Is Important

The Challenge

Every owner and director must ask her- or himself, "What is the purpose of this center? Is it to provide day care, make money, or care for children?"

Solutions

I decided I needed a vision statement that expressed the purpose of our program. I started by thinking of key words that represented what we wanted to accomplish through our program. I also asked the staff to describe, in one sentence, what happened in our program. I wrote down all of the key words and sentences and in the end, I came up with the following finished product:

Our center understands that every child is a unique individual. The goal of our program is to encourage the social, emotional, physical, and cognitive development of each child. Parents are our partners as we work together to facilitate a developmentally appropriate environment that promotes learning. We are passionate about offering every child the opportunity to discover and understand their world through the life experiences they encounter at our center. We look forward to the memories children will develop as a result of their time in our program.

Once you have your vision statement, include it in every piece of literature you can. Display it all over your center. Have a copy framed and posted near the entrance of your center and in every classroom, including your office. Reading your vision statement often keeps your mind focused on why you do this work instead of on the problems you might be facing at the time. It also informs others visiting your program.

Key Points to Remember

◆ Create a vision statement; invite your staff's input.
◆ Share your vision statement as often as possible.
◆ Post your vision statement near the front door, in your office, and in every classroom.

For More Information

* For complete bibliography, see pages 209-217.

◆ Read one of my favorite books, *The Visionary Director* by Margie Carter and Deb Curtis.

How to Choose a Business Card, Letterhead, and Other Materials

The Challenge

I can remember when I got my first business card. I was so proud to see my name and title on the card with the school's name and logo. I immediately mailed a card to my dad, and I am sure he was so proud. At one of the centers where I worked, one of the things the board asked me to do was to revamp all of our stationery and company materials. I took on the task with passion.

Solutions

Because your business card, enrollment forms, and parent handbook are the first printed materials many people see, they need to make a professional impression. I have been to centers where the forms I received were run off on the copier and looked as if the person did not even know how to run a copier—they looked very unprofessional, to say the least. In our technologically savvy world, you do not even have to hire a professional graphic artist to design your forms (unless you have a skilled parent in your program who is willing to donate his or her time). You can design your own forms using a computer and some good software.

Choose a logo that you feel represents your program. Your logo should be on every piece of literature you distribute, so make sure you really like it. Work with your graphic artist or find a good clip art computer program and start designing. Once you have decided on your logo and have it in place, you can start really looking at your parent handbook and other forms. When was the last time they were updated? Have major policies and procedures changed? Are there typos that were never corrected? Once you make necessary changes, take time to review it. Ask several people to review it for typos and mistakes. Next, you need to get the new book/forms approved by the board and your center attorney. Once changes have been made and approved, proceed with printing.

Professional printing can be expensive, but if your center can afford it, it's a good idea. You will save money by printing forms you use often in bulk. Not every form needs to be professionally printed, though. Most of the day-to-day forms can be copied in your office. The key to clean copies is having a clean original

and a decent copier. I suggest keeping all of your original copies inside of sheet protectors in a three-ring binder. This keeps copies looking clean and professional. Also, having the originals in one place makes them easy for everyone to find.

Key Points to Remember

◆ Work with a graphic artist (or purchase a clip art program) to design a new logo for your business card, letterhead, and other office materials.
◆ Review all of your forms to see if changes need to be made.
◆ Make needed changes and create new forms, if necessary.
◆ Have the appropriate amounts printed.
◆ Use the new products with pride.

For More Information

* For complete bibliography, see pages 209-217.

◆ Read the article "Power Pack Your Center Brochure" by Julie Wassom in the July/August 2000 issue of *Child Care Information Exchange.*

How to Schedule Your Day

The Challenge

Directors often feel that there aren't enough hours in the day. Between phone calls, meetings, filling in for staff, and running in and out of classrooms, a normal workday can be "lost" putting out fires and handling unexpected situations.

Solutions

Schedule, schedule, schedule! Start by making a list of all the things you hope to accomplish in a day—check staffing pattern for the day, greet children, visit classrooms, facilitate tours, dispense medicine, return phone calls, and so on. Schedule these items to help you actually accomplish your goals. I am sure you have heard the saying, "If you fail to plan, then plan to fail." (I think it was written for center directors!) Of course, you might not actually fail as a director if you don't plan, but chances are you won't live up to your potential either. Keep a calendar that includes center events and holidays, staff absences, parent tours, class field trips, meetings, and other important details. This will help keep you from being caught by surprise and being unprepared. I suggest making daily, weekly, and monthly goals, then make your schedule from your goals. You will be amazed at what you can accomplish (see Sample Daily Schedule on page 204 in the Appendix). As you are planning your schedule, keep drop-off and pick-up times in mind. That is the time you want to be accessible to parents and teachers, not returning phone calls. Make a realistic schedule, one that works with the flow of your center. There were times I would slip out of the habit of scheduling and find myself in chaos mode. I would get in my car at the end of the day and think, "Did I accomplish anything today?" Try a few of these scheduling tips:

◆ Have a phone system in place (see How to Handle Phone Calls on page 117).

◆ Schedule an hour a day to return phone calls.

◆ Put a wipe-off/cork board combination outside your office door so people can leave notes when you are unavailable.

◆ Inform staff members and parents of your schedule. It helps hold you accountable, and it lets them know that time is important to you.

◆ Prioritize your day, scheduling the most important things first.

Key Points to Remember

◆ Schedule, schedule, schedule.

◆ Stick to your schedule.

For More Information

* For complete bibliography, see pages 209-217.

◆ Check out the website www.daytimer.com. It has everything you need to get organized. It also has great articles on time management.

◆ Another great way to save time is by using a book of forms. A good book to refer to is *The Boring Book of Forms, Volume I: Every Employee Form You Will Ever Need* by Elizabeth A.N. Powers, M.ED (upcoming title). Call the Georgia Association on Young Children at 404-222-0014, or visit www.gayconline.org.

How to Organize the Paper in Your Life

The Challenge

Bills, enrollment forms, accident reports, and sticky notes can take over your desk. I remember at times wondering if I even had a desk under all the paper!

Solutions

The simple trick to controlling paperwork is to handle it immediately. When the mail arrives, set aside 15 minutes and deal with it right away. Schedule 15 minutes every day to sort through the mail, answer what needs answering, and toss what needs tossing. I used to have a "to be filed" folder on my desk, and it quickly filled up. It would be better to go ahead and put the papers in the appropriate file than to let them pile up. Once that pile gets going, it is hard to take the time to knock it down.

Another trick is to take the last 10 minutes of every hour and clean up what you have been doing. I decided to try out this suggestion while I was writing this book. Every hour, I used the last 10 minutes and tossed or put away the research material I no longer needed, asked the children to retrieve all of the toys they had brought into my office, and threw away any trash that was on my desk. It really did work. I found myself working in a clean and enjoyable environment, and it was easier to get my hands on the research I did needed. Whenever I left my office and returned, it was tidy.

Key Points to Remember

◆ Handle paperwork immediately.
◆ Schedule 15 minutes per day to handle mail.
◆ Keep the piles to a minimum.
◆ Use the last 10 minutes of every hour to clean up and reorganize.

For More Information

* For complete bibliography, see pages 209-217.

◆ Read the article "Identifying What You Need in a Jungle of Paper Work" by Kim Mitcham in the March 2001 issue of *Child Care Business*. Call 480-990-1101 ext.1095 for a back issue.

How to Handle Phone Calls

The Challenge

I often felt overwhelmed by the number of phone calls I received. There were days when I felt like I was glued to the telephone receiver. At times, even the sound of the ringing can get on my nerves.

Solutions

Although I do not always feel that "new and improved" is better than the original, when it comes to voice-mail systems, I do. I remember when I made my first call to a center that had an automated voice-mail system. I was not sure if I liked it or not. I had questions, such as how could I get in touch with that person if it was an emergency? Would prospective parents be turned off by it? But as I listened, I realized the center had considered all of these things. Their message was similar to the following: "Thank you for calling Heritage Learning Center. Your call is important to us. If you would like to speak with the director, Diane, press 1; if you need to leave a message for another staff member, press 2; and if you need directions and tour times, press 3. Feel free to page us at 555-1245 if you need to speak with someone immediately." The message was clear, informative, and the tone was warm. I knew it helped the director manage phone time. If it was an emergency, someone could page her. If not, she could check and return calls according to her schedule (I am sure she had one). If you do use a voice-mail system, remember to check your messages several times a day.

If you want to manage your phone calls without using a voice-mail system, you have another option. You could hire someone to answer the phone and complete a few other administrative tasks. (This position can be called assistant to the director.) However, this option costs a little more money and takes more time. If that is not a problem for your center, it might be a great option for you. If you are available you can take the call. If not, ask the assistant to take messages, which allows you to return the call during your scheduled phone time.

Either way, you will be amazed at the amount of time you can save by not stopping to answer the phone. However, make sure staff members know how to get in touch with you. For example, you don't want to make it too convenient for a staff member to call in sick by leaving a message. It's a good idea to make it a policy that absences, tardiness, and other situations that require a conversation with you will be unexcused unless the staff member has spoken directly with you.

Key Points to Remember

◆ Consider having an automated voice-mail system or receptionist/assistant to answer the phone.

◆ Schedule a time to return phone calls.

◆ Return phone calls in a timely manner.

For More Information

* For complete bibliography, see pages 209-217.

◆ Read *Smart Questions: A New Strategy for Successful Managers* by Dorothy Leeds.

How to Create a Website for Your Center

The Challenge

I recently faced this challenge myself. I wanted to develop a website for my business and did not know where to begin.

Solutions

First, I went on the Internet. I did a search for preschools, childcare centers, early childhood organizations, and authors/trainers. Next, I read magazine articles, and asked everyone I knew about their own websites or websites they liked. After many hours searching the Internet and many conversations about this subject, I decided that it was worth the time and effort to pursue.

You might ask, why does my center need a website? My answer is that it can improve communication. Think about how easy it would be for parents to go to your center's website and read the monthly newsletter, their child's classroom letter, the school calendar, reminders about payment, school closings, and other school-related details. A website has the potential to fill so many communication gaps. In addition, it is an excellent marketing tool. You could have a page for prospective parents that includes general information about the program. It is also a good idea to have a separate, members-only page for enrolled families. This way parents will be the only ones who can access such things as school events or other private information.

How do you create a website? This is a complicated question, but there are many ways to go about it. There are websites that lead you through creating simple websites:

www.teacherweb.com
www.createawebsite.net
www.make-a-web-site.com
www.earthlinkhosting.net

You could also take a website design class that will help you learn all you need to create your own site. You can purchase web design software to help you manage your site, or hire a graphic artist/web designer to handle it all for you. The route you choose

depends on your computer abilities, your time, and your financial resources. After you have created your website, you will need to update information occasionally. A good resource for updating your website is Microsoft Front Page.

Key Points to Remember

◆   Decide if a website is right for your center.
◆   Research the Internet and find sites you like.
◆   Decide what route you will take to create your website.

For More Information

* For complete bibliography, see pages 209-217.

◆   The following articles are excellent resources:
"The Way of the Web" by Julie Wassom in the May/June 2002 issue of *Child Care Information Exchange*
"Internet as a Relevant Marketing Tool" by Ken Miles in the Aug/Sept 2000 issue of *Child Care Business Magazine* (Call 480-990-1101 ext.1095 for a copy of this issue.)
"Welcome to the World of the Web" by Renee Targos in the November 2000 issue of *Child Care Business*
◆   ART Enterprises is the company I used to design my website. Check out www.earlychildhoodresources.com or www.artenterprises.com. You can also call 770-664-6261 for more information.

Why It's Important to Know Your Strengths and Weaknesses

The Challenge

I am definitely a "people person." I love giving parents tours around the center, meeting with staff, and generally anything that involves people. However, it is difficult for me to be alone and work on any task-oriented project. I tend to procrastinate about anything that involves paper and quiet time.

Solutions

The thing that helps me handle my strengths and weaknesses is that I know what they are. I can identify the things that I am good at and the areas where I need some improvement. There are all sorts of ways to identify your strengths and weaknesses. Try taking a personality test or management quiz to figure out the areas in which you excel and those that need some work.

Once you identify your weaknesses, make a plan. For example, if you are terrible at returning phone calls, ask someone to hold you accountable. If you procrastinate with your paperwork (like me!), schedule it into your day and stick to it. Close your door and stay in your office until you get it done. You might want to take a course or attend a workshop that addresses the area of your weakness. Remember, no one is perfect and being who you are is what makes our world an interesting place to be.

Key Points to Remember

◆ Identify your strengths and weaknesses.
◆ Develop a plan to address your weaknesses.
◆ Find someone to hold you accountable.

For More Information

* For complete bibliography, see pages 209-217.

◆ Visit the website www.kolbe.com and take the Kolbe Index.
◆ Read the article "How Are You Doing? A Center Director Self-Review Tool" by Karen L. Talley in the Sept/Oct 1997 issue of *Child Care Information Exchange*. After you have finished the article, send out the included survey to your staff.

How to Network

The Challenge

When I first moved to Atlanta, I struggled with the feeling that I was alone in this childcare world. I had just moved from Texas, where I worked for a private company that owned many centers. The big advantage to that was the support I received from other directors in the company. Even though I loved my new job, I longed to talk to someone in my field about the issues I was facing.

Solutions

Fortunately, I received a phone call from a director who was close by. Ann knew that I was the new director of a church childcare center, so she invited me to a meeting for church childcare directors. I was very thankful for her kindness. Because of my personality (remember, I'm a people person), I was not intimidated by meeting a new group of people. I walked up and introduced myself to almost everyone there. I still keep in touch with many of the directors I met at that first meeting more than 10 years ago.

I think networking is one of the keys to having a successful program and being a successful director. Try to get to know the center directors at the five closest programs. Be the initiator; invite them over for coffee one morning. If there is no network in place, share your desire to develop a networking group and invite them to be a part of it. Hopefully, the group of directors will become mentors, supporters, and allies. I called my neighbor directors to let them know when I had openings, when I needed staff, or when I had a great candidate that I didn't need. I called to compare prices, ratios, and services offered. It may seem crazy for me to suggest that you work with the directors who manage centers that compete for your business. But remember, if you are offering the best program you can, the parents at your center will want to be there. Also, once you realize that your center cannot meet the needs of every family, you might actually send some of those directors business (and vice versa).

Networking definitely goes beyond area directors. Whenever I attend conferences, seminars, or other early childhood meetings, I make it a goal to meet at least two new people. I take my business cards and expect to hand them out. You never know when networking will pay off. When I worked in Texas, I attended the NAEYC conference held in New Orleans that year. I attended a seminar on resource and referral and I was very impressed with the presenter. I introduced myself to the presenter after the seminar and thanked her for sharing her knowledge. About six months later, my husband and I moved to Atlanta and I needed a job. I thought about people I had ever met in the field from Atlanta and this presenter came to mind. I always saved my NAEYC program because it contained a lot of information, including this person's name and number. I called her and explained that I had attended her session and was very impressed by what she had to say. She offered to meet with me and help me find a job. Guess what? She did!

Time and time again, networking has paid off for me. I really understand why people say it is not what you know, but who you know that gets you what you want. I prefer to think it is a nice balance of both. I understand that for some people, walking up to strangers and introducing themselves might be like asking them to jump off a bridge. If you find it hard to do this, start small. When you attend meetings, try to meet one new person. If you are lucky, he or she will initiate the conversation.

Key Points to Remember

- Attend local early childhood meetings, and try to meet at least one new person.
- Visit the five closest centers to meet the directors.
- Invite the five nearest directors to your center for coffee.
- Start a director's network with any of the five that are interested.

For More Information

* For complete bibliography, see pages 209-217.

- A good article to read that addresses this issue is "A Director's Lot Is Not a Happy Lot" by Henry M. Morgan in the January 2001 issue of *Child Care Information Exchange*.
- Go online and join an administrator's newsgroup. The website www.geocities.com/Athens/Forum/5274/loops.html provides a list of newsgroups you might want to join.

How to Conduct Center Evaluations

The Challenge

I find it difficult to ask people what they think about my work. Therefore, asking parents to complete surveys evaluating our center was tough. I always assumed that the only people who would complete an evaluation survey would be those who had issues with my center.

Solutions

In spite of how I felt, I knew I needed to make parent evaluations part of my yearly plan (see Sample Yearly Parent Survey on page 183 in the Appendix). Allowing the parents to express their honest opinions about their child's program and "home away from home" lets them know you value their input. Following are some tips to use regarding parent evaluations:

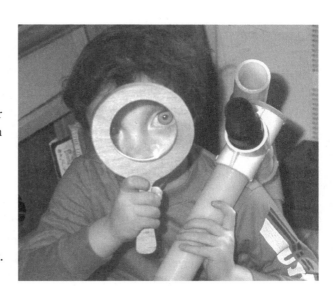

◆ Offer surveys on a yearly basis.

◆ Allow surveys to be anonymous. You will get the most honest answers this way. However, do not be surprised if quite a few parents sign their names. Some people will want you to know who said what.

◆ Allow room for a comment section at the end of the survey. Many parents will want to give specific feedback on their survey.

◆ Make a big deal of surveys. I usually stood in the hallway with donuts and coffee every morning for a week in hopes of getting the best response. It worked—usually about 75%-80% of the parents responded.

◆ Review all surveys. Don't lose heart if not every survey is positive; instead, try to look at it from the parent's perspective.

◆ Once you have read through all of the surveys, acknowledge your appreciation to parents for taking the time to complete the survey. Assure them that you and the other office staff will consider everything that was mentioned in the surveys.

◆ Inform parents of changes that will be made as a result of the surveys.

◆ Meet with individual parents or a group of parents if they would like to discuss anything on the survey.

◆ Go ahead and let out that sigh of relief. You don't have to read this page again until next year!

Key Points to Remember

◆ Make surveys a part of your yearly plan.

◆ Encourage parents to complete a survey by offering an incentive, such as coffee and donuts.

◆ Inform parents of changes you plan to make as a result of the survey.

For More Information

* For complete bibliography, see pages 209-217.

◆ *Taking Stock* by Roger Neugebauer (editor) is a helpful book.

Why Budgeting and Other Money-Saving Tips Are Important

The Challenge

Don't you wish money really did grow on trees? I have spent many hours dreaming for a big oak tree with large bills on it. Unfortunately, I wake from my dream with my checkbook and bills in front of me instead of money trees. One of the challenges directors face is making sure there is enough money to cover all of the center's expenses.

Solutions

The first step is committing yourself to making a budget. I know some of you might be thinking that you are not an accountant, but you can do this! Start by tracking your income and spending for a month. How much tuition income do you receive each month? How much do you spend on snacks, materials, and payroll each month? This will give you some idea of how much is coming in and how much is going out. When figuring your tuition budget for a year, keep in mind that you will have weeks without full tuition. Children leaving throughout the year and empty spaces are the main causes for less than full tuition income. I usually budgeted at 85% capacity when figuring tuition income for the year. The majority of expenditures will be for payroll. I remember the first time I saw my payroll figure—I almost passed out! If your payroll figure does not make you a little "sick," you are probably not paying your staff enough.

Here are some money-saving tricks I have learned along the way:

◆ Start a reasonable budget—It is better to find yourself with money left over at the end of the year than bouncing checks.

◆ Don't be afraid to ask—You will be surprised at what people are willing to donate. From parents to local businesses, many people may be excited about donating materials and time to your center.

◆ Recycle—So many items can be used again and again. Scraps of paper can be cut up for collage materials, and empty wipes containers make great toddler toys or storage containers for markers and other materials. Have a contest among your staff to find the most creative uses for recycled items.

◆ Allow staff to leave—During holidays and other low attendance times, offer staff members a chance to go home early. Instead of hiring substitutes, try to move staff around to cover rooms. I am NOT suggesting you take away staff from a room when they are needed; I am suggesting doing this ONLY when numbers are low and the staff are not needed. Most teachers are very willing to help out in a pinch.

◆ Switch things around from room to room—A great way to keep things fresh in the classroom is to change the items in it. However, this can be quite expensive. So instead of buying kitchen equipment for all of your classrooms, buy it for a few. For the other rooms, buy housekeeping equipment, such as a playhouse, cabin, or boat, or a sofa and rocking chair. Move the furniture equipment to a new classroom every six weeks. This keeps children interested, and lets you save a lot of money!

◆ Sharing is our friend—If you were to inventory every classroom, what would you find? Probably lots of stuff that should be kept in the resource room for everyone to share. Money is often spent duplicating items you already have but can't seem to find. Helping staff get into a routine of returning items to the resource room can save lots of money.

◆ Did I mention, don't be afraid to ask—I thought it was worth saying twice!

◆ One more budgeting tip—When you write a check, do not forget to take it out of the budget. Code every penny spent, and you will not have a nightmare on your hands when balancing your budget.

Key Points to Remember

◆ Start with a reasonable budget.
◆ Code every purchase made.
◆ Follow the money-saving tips mentioned above and develop your own!

For More Information

* For complete bibliography, see pages 209-217.

◆ Check out the books *Financial Management for the Childcare Executive Officer* by Karen Foster-Jorgenson with Angela Harrington, and *The Bottom Line for Children's Programs* by Gwen Morgan.

How to Conduct Room Observations

The Challenge

Do you know what really goes on in the classrooms in your center? You may see lesson plans, but are you sure of how the teacher communicates with the children? You may see artwork hanging on the walls, but when is it done and who actually does it? If a parent asks you about his or her son's teacher and her discipline style, will you be able to answer?

Solutions

You must have room observations. The solution to this challenge is simple, but implementing it is difficult. Room observations are a must in any quality program. The director has to know what is going on in order to effectively manage the center. The difficult part is finding time to get into the classrooms long enough to observe. Here is my solution for you: the critical **15 minutes**. Spend 15 minutes in each classroom writing down everything you see during that time. Do not worry about analyzing what you are seeing, just write it down. If you have

10 classrooms to observe, you will have 2 ½ hours of observation. You can find 2 ½ hours in your day! Remember, schedule it, write it on the calendar, and stick to it.

Let staff members know that you will be conducting observations on a regular basis. Once again this serves as a reminder to them, and makes you accountable. After you have observed each classroom, take the time to go over your observation with the teachers in the room. Simply share what you observed and give the teacher the chance to add to and explain your observations. If something does need to be addressed, then do so, and develop a plan to fix it. End the observation meeting with something positive and thank the teachers for their efforts. This should take about the same amount of time as the observation—15 minutes for each classroom.

Consider observing one week, meeting with teachers the following week, then observing the next week again, and so on. This type of schedule is very workable and allows teachers a week

in between to work on any previous issues. When you first begin room observations, you might want to try observing and meeting just once a month. Even then, you will notice a BIG difference in your program. The staff will look forward to your visit and respect you for taking the time to be in their classrooms.

Key Points to Remember

♦ Make a plan for classroom observations, schedule them, and stick to the plan.
♦ Observe in each classroom following the 15-minute plan.
♦ Meet with staff to review the observation.

For More Information

* For complete bibliography, see pages 209-217.

♦ *The Power of Observation* by Judy Jablon, Amy Laura Dombro, and Margo Dichtelmiller is a great book to read on the topic.
♦ Check out the video, *Observing Young Children* by Teaching Strategies. Contact www.teachingstrategies.com.
♦ Read the book *I Spy Something* by Ann Marie Leonard.

How to Create an Inviting Office Space

The Challenge

Has a visitor ever dropped in for a meeting, and then been unable to sit down until you cleared a space? This happened to me, and it was very embarrassing.

Solutions

When a prospective or enrolled parent enters your office, he or she should see a professional representation of you and the center. Look at your office and ask yourself if it represents you well. I decided to change my office from a cluttered junk room to a comfortable, inviting place. Keeping your office tidy is another important part of creating an inviting environment. I started by cleaning out the junk, going through paperwork, and packing up unnecessary items. To keep my office clean, I practiced the 15-minute rule. Before I left my office at the end of the day, I would use the last 15 minutes to tidy up for the next day. I would make sure the floor was free of clutter and my desk was organized (there may have been a lot of stacks, but they were organized!). This made a huge difference in my attitude when I walked in the next morning. Many times the director's office can become the drop-off place for everything; therefore, having a storage area other than your office can be a great organizing tool.

To make my office warm and inviting, I brought in a few things from home—a small table and lamp, a candle, and a candy dish. I also decided to rearrange the furniture. Before I rearranged, parents and staff sat in the two chairs I had in front of my desk. I felt that the desk served as a barrier between me and the parent or staff member, and I wanted to change that. I found a way to move my desk so that I when I turned my seat to the left, I would be facing the two chairs. I placed my slightly worn little table from home between the two chairs, and I put the lamp, candle, and candy dish on top. I filled the candy dish with chocolate and mints for guests. I love candles, and I believe the smell of a candle can really soften the environment. Many days I would turn off the bright fluorescent lighting and use the soft light from two lamps and a candle. It turned out to be quite cozy.

Key Points to Remember

◆   Evaluate your office space.
◆   Design a comfortable space that can accommodate parents and staff during meetings.
◆   Rearrange your office to help accomplish your goals.
◆   Accent with accessories that complement your new, soft look.
◆   Keep your office organized and clutter-free.
◆   Use the last 15 minutes of your day to tidy up your office.

For More Information

* For complete bibliography, see pages 209-217.

◆   Visit the website, www.homefurnish.com/deco3.htm#cozy, for some practical ideas as you create a cozy office.
◆   Look at decorating magazines for ideas.

How to Have an Effective Board of Directors

The Challenge

A board of directors governs many businesses, including childcare centers. The trick is to help board members understand both their role in the center and the theories of child development.

Solutions

There are two types of boards: a policy-making board and a working board. I have worked with both types, and each has their strengths and weaknesses.

A policy-only board does not get involved in the day-to-day operations and usually meets once a quarter to discuss and set policies. When I worked at a program that was governed by a policy-making board, it consisted of two parents, two church members, two members from the community, and the minister of education. The board received financial statements each quarter prior to the board meeting and any issues were discussed at that time. Enrollment and pertinent staff or parent issues might also be discussed during a board meeting. Once a year I submitted my budget proposal for approval. The board was ultimately responsible, so they needed to know what was happening with the money. However, it was up to the director to handle the day-to-day aspects of the finances. The only hiring for which the board was responsible was that of the administrative team. For example, when an assistant director left, the board created a search committee and together we interviewed and hired a new assistant director. With a policy-making board, the director handles most things independently with the exception of policies, and involves the board only when necessary.

On the other hand, a working board is very involved. Each board member has a specific role, usually chairing a committee that helps the director. There are usually personnel, finance, facilities, and special events committees. Some centers also have a ways-and-means committee, a public relations committee, and a parent representative to the board. Each board member is responsible for his or her area. For example, when I worked with this type of board, I wrote checks and coded them, but the finance board member did the rest. He balanced the books and prepared the budget. I had input, but he did the work. The head of the personnel committee sat in on many of the interviews and had a say in the actual hiring. The director did have ultimate authority, but there were more people involved in many of the decisions regarding the center. While there are many advantages to this setup, it was definitely more challenging to have to work with several people to get one thing accomplished.

No matter what type of board you are working with, the members need to have some training. Most board members do not have an early childhood background and need to be educated on the basic theories. I suggest this be done during an annual retreat-type meeting. A Friday evening and Saturday morning is ideal. However, any time the board can meet will work. If your budget can afford it, hire a speaker. If not, consider trading off with another director. You can speak at her board meeting and ask her to speak at yours. I am sure you and your colleagues have plenty of knowledge to share with the board members. Take time to communicate your vision and purpose for the program. Have the board members work in groups to form their goals for supporting the center during the upcoming year. End the retreat by challenging the board members to be committed to your program and to work together throughout the year.

Key Points to Remember

- ◆ Identify the type of board of directors your center has (or will have)—a policy-making board or working board.
- ◆ Plan a board retreat.
- ◆ Make a commitment to work together throughout the year.

For More Information

* For complete bibliography, see pages 209-217.

- ◆ Read the article "Orienting and Evaluating Your Board of Directors—Keys to Effective Board Management" by Gary Bess and Cindy Ratekin in the Nov/Dec 2000 issue of *Child Care Information Exchange*.

How to Address Director Burnout

The Challenge

At times, I felt like screaming, "Take me away!" As you probably know, the life of a director is far from relaxing or glamorous. Burnout is a very real problem.

Solutions

Being aware of burnout is the first step to rejuvenation. Whenever I was at my lowest point, I found myself heading to the baby or toddler room for some unconditional love. In that room, it did not take long for a smile to return to my face. However, I needed a long-term solution. I visited with other colleagues and shared "war" stories. I had always been aware of teacher burnout and how to prevent it, but I had not thought about preventing director burnout. I came up with the following plan to blow out burnout:

- Get involved in an early childhood group. Your local NAEYC chapter is a great resource. The support you receive there can be critical.
- Schedule some time away from the center once a month to catch up on some reading. Go have coffee at a local coffee shop with a few journals or a good book. (I mean early childhood materials, not a novel!)
- Put money in the budget for training. There are many great conferences available; take advantage of them. Try to plan one conference away from your city at least once a year. At least every other year attend a leadership conference.
- Rest when you need it. Don't underestimate the power of rest and relaxation.
- Develop a support system. Get to know several directors who can support you and whom you can support. There is something to be said for having people around who can understand the stresses and strains of your profession.
- Spend time on your hobby. Just like staff members, directors need to balance their work and home life. Play is powerful. Do you have a hobby? Mine is faux finishing furniture.

Key Points to Remember

- Be aware that you are not immune to burnout.
- Follow the "blow out plan" mentioned above.

For More Information

* For complete bibliography, see pages 209-217.

- Read the following books: *Lifesavers: Tips for Success* and *Sanity for Early Childhood Managers* by Sue Baldwin, Mary S. Whelan (editors), and *Lighten Up and Live Longer: A Collection of Jokes, Anecdotes, and Stories Guaranteed to Tickle Your Soul* by Robert A. Wray and Sue Baldwin.
- Check out your local parks and recreation brochure, your community college catalogue, or a good book to pursue your hobby.
- Read the article "Paralyzed by Personal Stress" by Suzanne Gellens in the Sept/Oct 1994 issue of *Child Care Information Exchange*.

How to Create Memories for the Director

The Challenge

Most of the time, the people who come to your office are adults—either parents or staff. However, children also come. Can you use your office to make memories for them and for you? Yes, you can.

Solutions

Many memories can be made in the office for both the director and the children. Most of the time children come to your office when they are sick or their parents are late. Take advantage of these times with individual children. Children will enjoy one-on-one conversation with you, and you will enjoy it too. Ask the children to draw pictures for you and post them in the office. Children will enjoy visiting and reviewing their work. Keep a box of special toys for your special visitors to enjoy during the visit. I also kept a basket of some of my favorite children's books. When a child is sick, most of them want to be held. Take advantage of this opportunity when you have it.

Memories can also be made outside the office. One of my favorite memories involved Michael, the little boy I talked about earlier (see page 74). Michael's mom needed to go out of town for work, and I offered to have him spend the night at my house. (This kind of situation did not happen often.) This was before I had children of my own, so it was a real treat for me to have a child in my home. We enjoyed playing in my yard and digging for worms. My husband and I took Michael out to dinner and shared some great conversation with this little four-year-old. He spent his time telling us about his recent trip to Disney World and how much fun he had with his mom. We had a great time. Little did I know that less than two months later Michael's life would end. He would not make any more memories, and we would not have the opportunity to make any new memories with him. I will always treasure the memories I have, especially when he was in my home. After he died, I renewed my vision for memory-making experiences in our program as often as possible.

Key Points to Remember

◆ Make your office a memory-making place.
◆ Encourage children to provide artwork for your office.
◆ Keep a box of special toys for children who visit.
◆ Look for other opportunities to make memories with children.

For More Information

* For complete bibliography, see pages 209-217.

◆ Check out www.turnthepage.com for a great list of children's books for your office.

Challenges Related to the Center

CHAPTER 5

How to Create Inviting Smells

The Challenge

Nothing is worse than walking into a center and smelling strong odors, such as bodily waste (dirty diapers), bleach solution, or fish sticks. Considering all the diapers that must be changed and the food that must be cooked, how can you keep your center smelling fresh and inviting?

Solutions

Smells are linked to memories, and who wants to remember smelly diapers? When I was working on this section, I asked my mom and her sister what smells they like. Naturally, neither said dirty diapers or bleach. My Aunt Paula loves the smell of spices and fresh pies or cakes. My mom likes fresh cut grass and the rain, but her favorite is a freshly bathed baby lathered with baby lotion. When I asked them what their favorite smell was, they answered my question without hesitation. Smells create strong memories. The children in your program will grow up and remember the smells of their childhood.

Baking bread is a simple way to help your center smell nice. Bread machines are very reasonable in terms of cost. With adult assistance and supervision, children can take turns adding ingredients into the machine. Boiling cinnamon sticks and other spices in the kitchen will also fill your center with pleasant smells. (Be sure to keep hot or dangerous sources of "good smells" away from children.) Companies are always coming up with new products to help places smell better. For example, plug-in air fresheners are a good idea.

When using fragrance sprays and room air fresheners, it's a good idea to stick with a light, clean smell instead of floral or musk. This will keep things smelling fresh instead of smelling like floral "poop." Don't mix smells; instead, buy several of one kind and if you want something different, switch after you run out.

The above solutions will help mask center odors. However, it's important to try to eliminate the offensive odors. Take dirty diapers outside of the building as often as possible. Keep potty areas clean and free from odor. Remember, walls and floors tend to get wet, especially when children are just learning to potty.

If you find yourself wondering how your center really smells, invite a friend or family member into your center. It's important to ask someone who is not there on a regular basis and who will give you an honest opinion.

Key Points to Remember

- "Smell up" your center with good smells.
- Assess how good or bad your center smells.

For More Information

* For complete bibliography, see pages 209-217.

- Check out www.breadbeckers.com to find out more on baking bread. This company even sells wheat grinders for centers who want to make their own bread from the wheat kernels.
- Read *Science Fair Success With Scents, Aromas, and Smells* by Thomas R. Rybolt and Leah M. Rybolt. This is a fun book that explains different science projects based on the sense of smell. It really helps you "smell" differently.

How to Help Teachers Learn to Share Materials and Resources

The Challenge

This subject can cause stress in any director's life. Most teachers seem to do a better job at encouraging children to share than sharing among themselves.

Solutions

From the beginning, I made it clear to the staff that I wanted them to have the space and materials they needed to facilitate an exceptional program for young children. I let them know that I budgeted money so that every classroom had enough quality materials. That said, I also reminded staff that everyone must work together to manage and share the space and materials. This all sounds good, and it worked most of the time. However, for those teachers who like to keep all their stuff buried in the closet for years and years, I have a solution.

Once a year, we closed the center for a teacher work day. The week before the work day, I asked the staff members to start cleaning out their rooms, removing all unnecessary items, such as the extra gallon of glue, the piles of newspapers, and other miscellaneous materials. If the items had a home in the resource room, then teachers were encouraged to put them back. If not, the staff lounge became the overflow room for the week. By Thursday evening everything except furniture, carpets, and personal belongings that the teacher purchased had to be removed from the classroom. Yes, everything. I had categories labeled in the hallway and staff members were to put their "stuff" in the appropriate category. After everyone's room was clean we did a walk through, checking off each room. This was done as part of the staff meeting for that month. That night the janitorial staff gave the rooms a nice cleaning so the staff could make a fresh start in the morning. On Friday morning, the teachers started by assessing their needs for their classroom. How many dolls do I really need? How many paintbrushes? How many puzzles? They made a list of items they needed and the assistant director or I helped them "shop."

I also budgeted money for some new materials every year, and I made sure to buy something new for each classroom. The teachers gave me a wish list and I worked from that. By Monday, all of the rooms were put back together looking fresh and clean. The children were excited to see their "new" room. The best part was knowing that everyone had to share.

Key Points to Remember

- Make it clear that you want the staff to have what they need.
- In order to do so, everyone must be willing to "let go" and share.
- Have a teacher work day once a year and clean out the classrooms.
- Rearrange the room and fill it with some different materials.

For More Information

* For complete bibliography, see pages 209-217.

- Check out the article, "Moving Staff Through Difficult Issues" in the July/August 2002 issue of *Child Care Information Exchange.*

How to Help Teachers Share Space

The Challenge

Some teachers may have difficulties sharing the playground or other common areas in the center.

Solutions

Let's start with the core of shared space issues. Communication is KEY! It is imperative to sit down with everyone involved and work out a plan. For example, when I was a director in a church program, we shared our space with the Sunday school. Every Monday, many teachers would be upset because the Sunday school teachers would move things around. In addition, some of the Sunday school teachers would leave notes asking us to leave an empty bulletin board or wall

space for them to use. Of course, the staff members in my program were upset. It appeared both had valid points and neither wanted to share.

I decided to invite all of the Sunday school teachers to dinner at the center to get to know the teachers in my program and vice versa. I assigned seats according to the rooms they shared. I thought it was important that we knew whom we were sharing our space with. I facilitated an ice breaker to help the groups feel more comfortable with each other, and then I gave each group assignments to work on together. The assignment was first to tell why they worked or volunteered in the positions they held. Next I asked them to share their goals for children using the space and then for the space itself.

I admit that not everyone's goals meshed, but this started a good discussion. By the end of the evening, the Sunday school and childcare teachers decided what needed to be put away before Sunday and what would be put back before Monday. They also decided how to handle the bulletin board issue. Most childcare teachers were willing to put a piece of blank butcher paper over their bulletin board for the teacher to use on Sunday. The Sunday school teacher was willing to take a few minutes every week and display what he or she needed for the lesson instead of leaving it up all week.

I also asked my teachers to volunteer one Sunday during the year to work in their room with the Sunday school teachers. Why? To help the childcare teachers connect with the children who were sharing their space. Although I did not ask the Sunday school teachers to reciprocate, many of them did. I was pleasantly surprised by the results of this dinner. From time to time, I encouraged the staff members to leave notes of appreciation and encouragement for the Sunday school teachers.

Key Points to Remember

- Communication is key.
- Have a meeting with everyone involved in sharing space.
- Encourage teamwork.
- Set the example.

For More Information

* For complete bibliography, see pages 209-217.

- Check out the website, www.elca.org/lp/preschl.html. This article discusses a director's relationship with the pastor, and there is a good reference to space issues.

The Importance of Room Arrangement

The Challenge

The way the room is arranged sets the tone of the classroom. The environment is the first step in facilitating learning. When rearranging a classroom, there are many decisions to be made.

Solutions

Let's start with the walls. Warm, neutral colors, such as khaki, taupe, or tan work best to create a natural setting in a classroom. Many times, people want to paint classroom walls bright colors thinking that children will enjoy them, but walls painted in bright colors can be over-stimulating. You can always paint the trim in the room with bright colors. Curtains or

window treatments are another good way to create a warm, inviting classroom. Plants are my favorite for creating a cozy space. Many plants need little light that can be hung out of the children's reach.

It is important to arrange a classroom based on the age group that uses it. Let's start with infants. What needs to be in an infant room? Soft floor spaces are a must. Babies need room to roll, crawl, pull up, and walk. Because teachers will be on the floor with the infants, their needs also must be considered when designing the infant room. Rocking chairs are another necessity for all infant rooms. However, you do not need one chair for every teacher because this discourages teachers from getting on the floor. It is much easier for a teacher to take care of several babies at a time when he or she is at their eye-level. What about all of the commercial baby "equipment"? You can get a few bouncy seats if you want, but floor time and sturdy furniture for pulling up is really the best "equipment" you can provide. This will save you a lot of money, too. Use the extra money to buy lots of unbreakable mirrors, which are an asset in a baby room (actually, any room). Use real pictures with infants. They are seeing so many things for the first time—it would be a shame for them to think a bear is a cute brown animal with a smile. Laminate the pictures and round the edges to handle all of the wear and tear of a baby room (not to mention the slobber!).

What about toddlers? Think BIG! Toddlers need to climb. Every toddler room should be equipped with some type of age-appropriate climbing equipment. The best way to get the most for your money is to buy two different types of climbers and rotate them between two rooms. This keeps the climbers fresh for the children. After the climber, move on to sensory materials. Providing plenty of sensory tubs and materials will really cut down on the aggression in a toddler classroom. Toddlers need to have their hands in and on things. Start displaying artwork at the children's eye level. Naturally, toddlers will want to pull their artwork off the wall, but you can encourage teachers to use this as a learning tool. They can remind toddlers over and over and over that pictures on the wall are for eyes only. Of course, teachers should not put their prized artwork on display. Instead, they can display artwork such as large sheets of butcher paper that the toddlers painted during outside time the day before. If it gets torn down, they can paint a new one tomorrow!

Preschoolers need a bit of everything. They need space for building—four-year-olds can build big buildings! They need space for talking. Consider adding some adult-size comfortable furniture for children to sit on to look at books with a teacher or to plan a birthday party with a friend. I know it is tempting for teachers to curl up on a comfy sofa, and I say if they are spending time with a child, great! Preschoolers also need plenty of space to create. Creating cards, pictures, and airplanes are all important at this age. Make sure each room is equipped with plenty of "stuff" for creating. Recyclables work great for this area.

I would be remiss if I did not mention including a space to be alone in every classroom, regardless of age. Each classroom should be equipped with a space where a child can take a break from the classroom and the people and noises in it. This can be made easily by cutting doors and windows into a large refrigerator box or by setting up a small tent with soft things inside.

Key Points to Remember

- Paint the walls a warm, neutral color.
- Use age-appropriate furniture throughout the room.
- Provide comfortable spaces.
- Decorate with realistic pictures at the children's eye level.
- Provide a space for children to be alone.

For More Information

* For complete bibliography, see pages 209-217.

- Read *Places for Childhoods: Making Quality Happen in the Real World* by Jim Greenman or *Early Learning Environments That Work* by Rebecca Isbell and Betty Exelby.

How to Keep the Center Clean

The Challenge

It is very important to keep your childcare center as clean as possible. The problem is how does one keep a building full of children clean?

Solutions

A clean center is very important. (However, the children's activities are often messy—and they should be because creativity and exploration "require" messes!) What must be kept clean are the floors, bathrooms, walls, and trash area. Teachers can and should clean and disinfect as they go, but if at all possible, a good janitorial service is key. Finding and training a quality cleaning crew can be a challenge. One way to help the cleaning staff is to ask them to read the state standards. After they read the standards, give them a tour of the center and highlight everything that is important to your program.

When I was a director, we invited the cleaning crew to a celebration for their hard work. The children made snacks and special pictures for the cleaning crew, and the cleaning crew moved from room to room to hear how their hard work was appreciated. It was great fun! It also helped the cleaning crew see that their hard work was for precious children. Sometimes centers think they will save money and ask the teachers to clean, but if financially feasible, having a cleaning crew is money well spent.

Key Points to Remember

- ◆ Hire a quality cleaning service. (Use your network of directors. See How to Network, page 121.)
- ◆ Tour the center with the crew, highlighting the problem areas.
- ◆ Invite the cleaning crew to a special lunch.
- ◆ Keep communicating with the crew.

For More Information

* For complete bibliography, see pages 209-217.

- Check your state licensing regulations for specifics.
- Call other directors to get referrals on a good cleaning company.
- Check the company's record by calling the Better Business Bureau at 703-276-0100 or on the web at www.betterbusinessbureau.org.

How to Create Inviting Spaces

The Challenge

Every childcare center has a different space—some have only one hallway, and others have several. No matter how big or small your space is, once families enter the front door you want them to feel welcome. How do you accomplish this?

Solutions

I think it is important for parents to feel welcome in the center as much as the children. Sometimes we get so involved in providing a cozy environment for children that we forget we serve parents too. My suggestion? Provide lots of inviting spaces in the hallways. Provide places for children to be with their parents during drop off, pick up, and special visits. I had a local carpenter make some simple benches, which I strategically placed throughout the center along with some oversized chairs. Ask parents to donate used furniture. Slipcovers can turn their slightly-worn-but-still-good furniture into something great and cozy. Next to the furniture I placed baskets of books for the families to enjoy. It was great walking down the hall seeing families enjoying books and special time together.

To take this a step further, don't forget to be welcoming to children's parents. I know I have mentioned the importance of greeting the children and calling them by name, but it is also important for the parents, too. Parents should feel that you are in the *family* care business, not just the childcare business.

Key Points to Remember

- Provide cozy furniture in the hallway and other common spaces.
- Provide baskets of books next to the furniture.
- Take time to greet parents when you see them in the hallway.

For More Information

* For complete bibliography, see pages 209-217.

◆ Read "Creating a Family-Like Atmosphere in Child Care Settings" by Linda C. Whitehead and Stacey I. Ginsberg in the March 1999 issue of *Young Children*.

◆ Read "Meeting Adult Needs Within the Classroom" by Eileen Eisenberg in the Sept/Oct 1997 issue of *Child Care Information Exchange*.

How to Handle the End-of-the-Day "Hungries"

The Challenge

Have you ever stood at the door during pick-up and counted how many children tell their parents they are hungry? I used to have parents stop by my office and ask if they could grab a cup of goldfish for the road. I traveled an hour to work, and I couldn't imagine traveling with a hungry child that far every day.

Solutions

First, I checked my budget to see if the center could provide a few extra snacks every week. Next, I surveyed parents to see if the majority of them would be interested in having a "to go" snack available for their children (see Sample "To Go" Snack Survey on page 205 in the Appendix). Overwhelmingly, the answer was yes. We purchased typical snack items and put them into snack-size baggies. We put the baggies in a big basket next to the front door in the afternoon so the children could take one for the ride home. It didn't take long for this snack area to become a hangout for families. Most of the children actually ate their snack while waiting for their parents to stop talking. When we started our "to go" snack program, I never imagined that it would be used to build community in our center. But that is what happened. It pleased me to see families chatting together every evening. On numerous occasions, parents would stop by the office and thank me for providing the snacks.

If your budget cannot handle more snacks, survey the parents again. Send out a letter explaining to parents that you want to start a "to go" snack basket for the children, but you need their help. Ask parents if they would be willing to buy an extra bag of goldfish crackers, dry cereal, raisins, animal crackers, or any other appropriate snack the next time they go to the store. Place a box in your office for donations. Most likely, the box will be filled in no time!

Key Points to Remember

◆ Survey parents to see if they are interested in having a "to go" snack.

◆ Check your budget to see if you can handle buying extra snacks. (Or, ask parents to pay a small extra fee or donate snacks for this service.)

◆ Provide snacks in small plastic baggies near the front door at pick-up times.

For More Information

* For complete bibliography, see pages 209-217.

◆ *Do Carrots Make You See Better?* by Julie Appleton, Nadine McCrea, and Carla Patterson is a great book for snack ideas as well as your entire food program.

Why Proper Signage Is Important

The Challenge

Signs, signs, everywhere; over here, over there! This sounds like a Dr. Seuss book, but having proper signage is important to every childcare center. How do you this?

Solutions

From your listing in the phone book to road signs to signs within the center, parents will appreciate your efforts. Let's start with placing an ad in the phone book. It's a good idea to pay for the smallest listing possible, making sure your address is correct. This way you can spend your money on more important things and people can get information from you, rather than a phone book advertisement.

Next, the signs outside of your center should clearly mark the parking areas and the entrance to the center. It is frustrating for prospective parents when they don't know where to go when they arrive. Once they have arrived at the entrance to the center, continue the signage. The office is usually the first place a visitor wants to find, so make sure it is marked well. Outside of each classroom, hang signs with the classroom

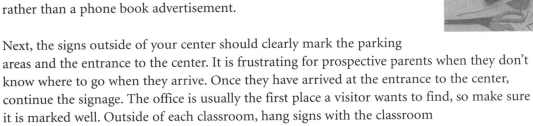

name and teacher bios, including pictures. This helps the parents get to know the entire staff and refreshes memories of teacher's names.

Make sure your exit signs are in the proper places. The fire inspector will let you know if you need more exit signs or if you need to move any of your current ones. Check them often to make sure the lights are working.

Key Points to Remember

◆   You cannot have enough signs!

For More Information

* For complete bibliography, see pages 209-217.

◆   Call several local sign companies and get an estimate for proper signage.
◆   www.fastsigns.com/products/banner is a national sign company with many locations.

Why the Outdoor Environment Is Important

The Challenge

So many times we worry about the classrooms inside the center and we forget about the outside environment. I remember when I mentioned to one of my staff members about evaluating our outside space, her comment was, "Why would we need to evaluate outside?"

Solutions

When I decided to evaluate our outside space, my first step was to involve the staff members. During a staff meeting, I asked the following questions and charted the answers.

1. What do you like about our outdoor space?
2. What do you wish was different about our outdoor space?
3. What do the children like most when they are outside?
4. What do the children like least when they are outside?

After reviewing the answers, we developed a plan. We decided that our basic equipment was fine. The children really enjoyed the climbing structures, but there is more to outside time than playground equipment. Believe it or not, there are some children who do not enjoy outside time. It's important to provide something for these children to do so that outside time will be something they look forward to, also. Books, art materials, dress-up clothes, and toy dinosaurs are just a start. (Remember, if things get dirty, they can be cleaned!) Take clipboards with paper and crayons outside for children to draw a nature picture or anything else from their imagination. Give them paper bags to collect objects from nature—these make great collage materials. Spray bottles, paint buckets and paintbrushes (to be used with water only), and large containers for bubbles are some of my favorite "wet" activities, great for a summer day. Some indoor classroom favorites, such as painting and blocks, can provide exceptional outside experiences as well.

Suggest that teachers create an "outside box" for their classroom. Each day the teacher and the children can choose different things from the box to take outside. Consider the children who don't typically like outside time. Ask them what they would like to do during outside time and try to provide it. It takes very little planning to move the indoors out, and the possibilities are endless.

Key Points to Remember

- Evaluate your outside environment.
- Ask the teachers for their opinions.
- Make a plan.
- Encourage teachers to take inside toys outdoors.

For More Information

* For complete bibliography, see pages 209-217.

- The May 2002 issue of *Young Children* contains seven relevant articles within a section entitled "Let's Go Outside!"
- Read "Environmental Education: A Walk in the Park Is Just the Beginning" by Carole Basile and Cameron White in the Summer 2000 issue of *Dimensions of Early Childhood*.
- Read *Hug a Tree* by Robert E. Rockwell, Elizabeth A. Sherwood, and Robert A. Williams.

How to Handle Security Issues

The Challenge

I always considered our center a safe place. We had keypads with codes and credit card entrances. Security guards that worked for the church were available for the child development center. We had a fire evacuation plan, and we even had a tornado plan. However, after September 11, I realized it was not enough.

Solutions

I called a friend who is a director and asked her how her center had handled security after 9/11. She told me that the center established a security committee to review and change the security procedures for the center. This committee researched the topic, and found the Georgia Emergency Management Agency (GEMA) to be very helpful. The security committee followed the guidelines laid out by this organization and made several changes to the existing policy. The committee developed a bombing plan, a disaster plan, portable emergency kits for each classroom (which contained a first aid kit and the children's emergency contact information), and specific location plans in case the center was destroyed so parents could find their children. It is scary to think about these issues, however, it is always better to be prepared. The center also chose to close down if there was an outside event that drew many people to the center. For example, on voting days the school was a voting site. Therefore, the center thought it would be in the children's best interest if it was closed.

Before 9/11, we were cautious and used security codes and locked doors. However, we were not "on edge" like many directors are today, especially in larger cities.

Key Points to Remember

- Invite parents to start a security committee.
- Provide them with appropriate websites or articles.
- Recommend any needed changes to the current policy.
- Implement changes.

For More Information

* For complete bibliography, see pages 209-217.

- http://www.gema.state.ga.us/ is one of many emergency information websites to review. Look for your state-based site. GEMA has a booklet on safety for childcare centers.
- Read "Securing Your Building" by Renee Targo in the June/July 2001 issue of *Child Care Business*. Go online to www.childcarebusiness.com for more information.

How to Create Memories for the Center

The Challenge

In the world of memories, I believe people remember the things around them in their "memory bank." I wanted the children in my program to have positive environmental memories in their bank.

Solutions

I decided that I was already offering a lot of great environmental memory opportunities with the good smells, inviting spaces, great teachers, and rich curriculum. However, I knew there was more that could be done. I decided to add small photo albums of the children to my basket of books in the hallway. This way the children could point out their friends to their parents. One year we dedicated an entire wall in the hallway to photos. We placed photos from the classrooms, field trips, staff events, and parent events throughout the year. We also invited parents to bring family photos from home to add to our wall. I would watch parents and children spend lots of time trying to find their family and friends on the wall.

Key Points to Remember

- Add small photo albums of the children to the hallway basket of books.
- Take lots and lots of pictures.
- Create a photo wall.

For More Information

* For complete bibliography, see pages 209-217.

◆ Check out *Time to Care: Redesigning Child Care to Promote Education, Support Families, and Build Communities* by Joan Lombardi.

Challenges Related to the Community

CHAPTER 6

How to Get to Know Your Community

The Challenge

If you are like me, during your work day you go to the same places for lunch, shop at the same stores, and drive by the same businesses on your way to work. Do you ever wonder who the people are that spend so much time practically next door to you? I did.

Solutions

I decided to meet the people in my neighborhood! I put together a packet of information to take to my neighbors. The packet included our brochure, my business card, a copy of our latest newsletter, artwork from a child in the center, and a letter expressing our desire to get to know them and be of service to them. I offered to provide artwork on a regular basis to display in the lobby or other central location of the business, and I invited the owners of the business to come by for a tour. I visited about 10 businesses including a doctor's office, a bakery, and a bank.

I did not know it at the time, but during my visits I had the opportunity to meet several prospective parents who worked near our center. One bank teller who was expecting a baby was unaware of our program. She interviewed me on the spot. A few months later, she came in for a tour and enrolled her daughter. The visits also allowed me to put names with

faces. When I went into the bakery, for example, I was able to say, "Good morning, Van" and make a personal connection with that business.

Taking the time to visit and meet the owners and employees of my neighborhood business paid off. We received many referrals from these businesses, provided artwork for several of them, and even received discounts on our purchases.

Key Points to Remember

◆ Put together a packet of information to take to businesses in your area.
◆ Take the packets to local businesses and introduce yourself.
◆ Enjoy the benefits of knowing your neighbors.

For More Information

* For complete bibliography, see pages 209-217.

◆ Call your local Chamber of Commerce to get the names and addresses of local businesses.
◆ Drive around and check out the businesses near you.
◆ Ask parents who live in the area where they like to conduct business.
◆ Read "Community Marketing Made Easy" by Julie Wassom in the May/June 2001 issue of *Child Care Information Exchange*.

How to Connect With the Community

The Challenge

Children brighten the day for so many people, including me. As directors, we get to be surrounded by kids and the "evidence" they leave behind. I wanted to spread that joy around in our community.

Solutions

I have already mentioned providing artwork for local businesses as a way to connect with the community. I received a lot of positive feedback from the businesses we worked with on this project. Each classroom would be responsible for one art project a month. We asked that the teacher make a sign explaining the artwork and giving credit to the artist. The artwork would be delivered to the business, the old artwork taken down, and the new artwork displayed professionally for the world to see. Many of the families lived near the center and visited these businesses regularly. Many parents told me how proud their children were when they saw their own artwork displayed somewhere other than school walls or the refrigerator at home. Some of the businesses that displayed our artwork included a retirement home, a fast food restaurant, and a family practice medical office.

Another way to connect with the community is to schedule field trips to the businesses in the area. Many businesses will allow groups of children to come in and look around as long as it fits into their schedule. For example, one of our preschool rooms went to the bakery and came back with lots of yummy pastries and chef's hats. The children talked about it for days. The business was rewarded by increased sales because the children begged their parents to go back. Another time, a group visited a retirement home close to our center. They scheduled the visit when there wasn't a major holiday and most residents probably wouldn't have many visitors. The children sang songs and gave the residents paper flower arrangements they made. The teachers took photographs of them with their new friends, which they later hung on the classroom wall. (The teachers also sent copies of the photos to the retirement home.) It was such a special visit that many other groups went to the same retirement home. Sometimes, nursing home environments may upset children, and some parents may have concerns about this type of event. In that case, try a different idea, such as going to a local farm or the studio of a local artist. The key is to keep your eyes and ears open for opportunities right outside your door.

Still another way to connect with the community is to offer your space to groups who might need a meeting place. For example, Brownie troops, home school groups, ballet classes, and piano lessons all need a location to meet. If space is available, let it be known that you are willing to help out by offering your space to others. You can mention it in your newsletter, and the word will spread. This says a lot about the value you place on sharing. You are speaking volumes with your actions. Of course, you will probably need to set specific guidelines, and you might even need to charge a reasonable fee for cleanup. You may or may not receive immediate benefits, but you are helping the community and the children in it.

A final idea on connecting with the community: Why not organize a group of parents and staff who are willing to work with an organization and invest some time and energy to build a house for someone who needs a home? What a great way to build a community among yourselves, while contributing to the community around you!

Key Points to Remember

◆ Display artwork at local businesses.

◆ Visit community businesses on a field trip.

◆ Offer your space to local groups.

◆ Build or renovate a house for someone in your community.

For More Information

* For complete bibliography, see pages 209-217.

◆ Read "Voices in Search of Cultural Continuity in Communities," a dialogue facilitated by Cecelia Alvarado in the Jan/Feb 2002 issue of *Child Care Information Exchange*.

◆ Check out www.habitat.org for more information on Habitat for Humanity.

How to Bring the Community to Your Program

The Challenge

Once, a parent asked me to consider banning field trips in our program. This got me thinking about how we handled our field trips and alternatives we could try.

Solutions

I really understood this parent's concerns. The day before, the news headlines read, "Child Dies in School Van." The story told how a teacher failed to count the children and check the van after returning from a field trip. The child had fallen asleep and died from the heat of a summer day. This tragedy understandably scared this mom.

After giving the issue much thought, I decided to continue field trips. After reviewing our policy, I created a field trip checklist that included writing each child's name on the form and accountability checkpoints (on the van, arriving at field trip, during the field trip, back on the van, arriving at the center, and safely in the classroom). (See Sample Field Trip Checklist on page 206 in the Appendix.)

I also created an alternative to going on field trips. We had field trips come to us! The following are some of my favorite field trips that can come to the classroom:

- ◆ Invite firefighters to bring their big, red fire engine to your school for a visit. They will likely oblige, unless there is an emergency that calls them away.
- ◆ Invite a chef to come in and make pancakes with the children one morning.
- ◆ Invite a veterinarian to bring in an animal and explain the responsibility involved in having a pet.
- ◆ Invite a dentist in for teeth-cleaning demonstrations to teach children how to care for their teeth.
- ◆ Invite a meteorologist in to discuss weather with older preschoolers and school-age children.
- ◆ Invite a florist in to make a floral arrangement with the children.
- ◆ Invite a soon-to-be mommy or a mommy with her new baby.
- ◆ Invite a parent in with his or her briefcase and suit.
- ◆ Invite an education representative from the zoo to bring in some animals.

This is just a beginning. Ask the children for more ideas.

Key Points to Remember

- ◆ Review your field trip plan.
- ◆ Check out field trips that can come to you.
- ◆ Ask the children for more ideas.

For More Information

  * For complete bibliography, see pages 209-217.

- ◆ A great article on neighborhood field trips can be found at:
    http://www.canr.uconn.edu/ces/child/newsarticles/FCC842.html

How to Start a Support Group

The Challenge

A childcare center is a natural place for people to connect. Whether it's for parents who are divorced, for grandparents raising their grandchildren, or for parents who have children with special needs, a support group can be extremely helpful.

Solutions

Starting a support group in your center could have a positive impact on the lives of many in your community. Many times, people are desperate to find others who share in their "unique" situation. Consider the following plan:

◆ Determine if there is a need for a support group. For example, if there are families in your center who are going through a divorce and they have asked you for help or guidance, ask if they would be interested in a support group.

◆ Invite one or two people to work with you on this task. Together, set goals and objectives for the group.

◆ Determine a meeting place, date, and time.

◆ Will there be a facilitator?

◆ Decide your ongoing involvement.

- Will this involve a professional counselor or simply support among peers?
- How many people will be in the group?
- What about childcare?
- Set an agenda.
- Design and print flyers to advertise the meeting. Put flyers up in other schools, churches, grocery stores, doctors' offices, and any of the other neighborhood businesses that know your center. Consider advertising in a local paper, on the radio, or on TV. Most offer free public service announcements.
- Have your first meeting. Introduce yourself and welcome others to your center.
- Continue listening to parents for new needs that may arise or how existing needs may change.

Key Points to Remember

- Determine if there is a need for a specific support group.
- Develop a plan to start a support group.
- Carry out your plan.

For More Information

* For complete bibliography, see pages 209-217.

- Check out this website for more information on starting a support group:
    http://www.parentsinc.org/newsletter/2001/supportgroup.html

How to Include the Community

The Challenge

I'm sure you have heard many questions from parents, such as "Where can I buy some of those puzzles like the ones in Grace's room?" "Do you know of a good family photographer?" "We need a new dentist, any suggestions?"

Solutions

Parents were always asking for names and phone numbers of businesses in the area. I decided we could help them and help ourselves at the same time. I looked for opportunities to offer advertisements in some of our printed materials. I decided on the parent handbook, the parent directory, and the parent newsletter.

Before I began soliciting local businesses, I asked staff members what ideas they had for how to use the money we would receive. We agreed to use it to pay for the printing of these materials and anything left over would go into a special fund for a piece of new equipment. Next, I needed to determine what I would offer as advertising options and fees. I decided to offer a business card, a half page, or an entire page as the options. I charged very reasonable fees because my main goal for doing this was to provide a list of resources for parents, not to make lots of money.

I was ready to advertise our idea. I decided to go to the parents first. Many of them worked in service-oriented businesses, and I thought they might like the opportunity to advertise. I was right. Several parents signed up. Next, I went to the same businesses I visited before and passed out an advertising flyer. Last, I approached vendors that the center used and asked them if they might be interested in advertising. We had a great response! We were able to cover our printing cost for all of these projects, plus have a little money left over. It really helped my budget, and we received many positive comments from the parents and advertisers.

Key Points to Remember

◆   Offer advertising in printed literature.

For More Information

* For complete bibliography, see pages 209-217.

◆   Contact your local NAEYC affiliate and speak with the person who handles advertising for them. Ask for information on rates, types of advertisers, and other pertinent questions.

◆   If any of the parents in your program work in advertising, use them as a resource.

How to Work With Other Programs

The Challenge

The Week of the Young Child is one of my favorite celebrations. I viewed it as a chance to get the word out that children are important. However, I needed help.

Solutions

I contacted several of the closest child development centers and invited the directors over for coffee. I shared my desire regarding The Week of the Young Child celebration and spreading the word in our community. I asked for input from the other directors. The following outlines our ideas for how we celebrated the week:

- Each center made a large banner with the title "The Week of the Young Child" and children put their handprints all over it. The banners were displayed in local businesses during that week.
- Each center provided two staff members to pass out literature on The Week of the Young Child at local businesses. (We paired teams from different centers to help teachers network.)
- Some of the classrooms from each center brought cookies and muffins packaged in small bags with "The Week of the Young Child" printed on them to the retirement homes in our area.

- Each center had its own celebration for the families. The celebrations varied from barbecue and pony rides to an art show and dessert.
- Each center made a photo album from the week and shared it with one of the other centers involved.

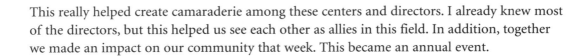

This really helped create camaraderie among these centers and directors. I already knew most of the directors, but this helped us see each other as allies in this field. In addition, together we made an impact on our community that week. This became an annual event.

Key Points to Remember

◆ Invite area directors to your center. (See information about networking with other directors on page 121.)
◆ Share your vision regarding The Week of the Young Child or other event.
◆ Together, create a plan for the celebration or event.
◆ Enjoy the camaraderie you have with these directors.

For More Information

* For complete bibliography, see pages 209-217.

◆ Visit www.naeyc.org for information about The Week of the Young Child.

How to Create Memories for the Community and the Children

The Challenge

What can we do to have an impact on the community? How can the community make an impact on the children?

Solutions

I came up with this memory-making idea for the children and for members of the community: "Read With a Grandparent." We invited grandparents from the community to come in and read with the children on a regular basis. We had several grandparents from the retirement home, some from a Sunday school class, and some of the children's actual grandparents visit the classrooms and read aloud. Some of the visitors enjoyed the baby room, while others headed down the hall to the preschoolers. It was such a rewarding experience for the children and the adults. I know many children (and adults) will carry memories of those special days with them forever.

In addition, we organized a community-wide event. Our center held an annual community event called the Spring Fling. This was the only real fundraising event we had each year and the money always went towards playground improvements. This was an event that required lots of work by parents and teachers. We offered games, rides, snacks, and a cakewalk. We attempted to get as much stuff donated for this event as possible. A local restaurant gave us a great deal on food, and we offered lunch for a reasonable cost. The event took place on a Saturday in late spring from 10:00 a.m. to 2:00 p.m. We advertised the event throughout the community and the turnout was amazing. The center staff wore our school T-shirts to help identify us in the crowd. We had many people from the community thank us for such a wonderful event. The event grew over the years and more booths were added and more people attended. It truly was a memory-making experience.

One of my favorite ideas for memory making with the community was Dad's Morning Out (with the children). We offered it twice a year on Saturday mornings and it was open to the community. We handed out flyers at stores and banks near our center. We asked teachers and parents to volunteer to help us offer games, activities, snacks, and story time for dads and their young children. This is a great time for dads to get away with the children for some quality time.

Another idea for making memories is to offer a book discussion group on a popular book about child rearing. You can pick the book or have the group decide what they would like to read and discuss. Lifelong friends and memories can often be made this way.

Key Points to Remember

◆ Develop community memory-making events, such as:
   –Sponsoring an annual community event.
   –Inviting grandparents into your center to read to the children on a regular basis.
   –Hosting a Dad's Morning Out.
   –Offering a book discussion group.

For More Information

* For complete bibliography, see pages 209-217.

◆ Check out your local *Kids* magazine. In the back there are usually advertisements for the equipment you may need for an annual community event such as a Spring Fling.

The
Preschool Director

Throughout this book, I focus on directors of childcare centers. However, after speaking with two friends who are directors of half-day preschool programs, I decided it was important to specifically address this group, too.

As a preschool director, you are in a unique position. You have just a few hours each day to offer a quality program that meets the needs of the children and the parents. Generally, two types of preschools are still functioning today: the church preschool and the co-op preschool.

The church preschool usually exists as a ministry of the church and functions under the church's umbrella. The co-op preschool is usually owned by the parents of the preschoolers or other organization and managed by the parents. The co-op approach requires a high level of parent involvement and commitment in order to function. Both types of preschools typically operate from 9:00am to 12:00pm and offer some extended care beyond 12:00pm. Because most preschools are half-day programs, you may not have to deal with such things as medication or naps. However, you face different challenges. Below, I will touch on some of these challenges, but for more in-depth information, use the list of resources at the end of this chapter.

Staffing

Staffing is a common issue for all directors (see How to Advertise for and Recruit Staff on page 9). Preschool directors have additional struggles. Finding qualified people who want to work part time and, therefore, do not need benefits can be a challenge. Co-op preschools I contacted use both teachers and parents to provide a quality experience for the children in their care. Parents are required to volunteer in a classroom on a regular basis, working with a qualified teacher.

Church preschools, on the other hand, rely on church members, mothers with young children, and neighbors and friends to find good staff. Church preschools also use parents as substitutes in the classrooms. As the director of a preschool, it is important to create an organized training plan for these teachers (see How to Train Staff on page 17). Whether you hire a trainer or take on the role yourself, make it a priority. When teachers are unprepared for the classroom, turnover rates increase. You can avoid this problem by training parents and staff properly, and their experience in the classroom is sure to be more rewarding for them and the children.

Expectations

Expectations can vary widely in a preschool setting. Some parents send their child to preschool as a preparatory class for kindergarten, while others hope their child will learn socialization skills. This wide range of expectations can be a challenge to you as a preschool director. The solution begins with having a clear picture of what it is that you actually offer. State your philosophy and vision statement in the parent handbook and display it throughout the center for parents to see on a regular basis.

Many parents are looking for a kindergarten preparatory school. A recent article in *USA Today** states that, "They (parents) are results-driven and want a great preschool for their kids." The article reports that years ago parents focused on their children getting into a "good" college so that a "good" job would follow, but that is no longer enough. Parents began to focus on getting their child into a "good" high school, and on down. Now many parents feel pressured into getting their child into a "good" preschool.

This poses the question: What defines a "good" preschool? I believe a good preschool is one that offers children the chance to discover, provides opportunities for children to explore and experience their world, and encourages a sense of wonder about the world. If that is your philosophy, can you meet the needs of a parent looking for an academic preschool? Sure. Educating parents is the key. Help parents understand that brain development is stimulated through touching, seeing, tasting, hearing, and smelling; and that words have value when they are read as books, told as stories, and sung as songs in the preschool classroom. Will their child learn to read by age three? Probably not. But will their three-year-old be a passionate life learner? I hope so. Parents' Night Out, as mentioned in How to Deal With the Academically Minded Parent on page 106, can be a helpful tool for you to use as part of orientation. This is a great way for parents to understand what your preschool is about.

*Della Cava, Marco, R. "Parents and Preschool: Schmooze or Lose." *USA Today*, August 28, 2002.

Money

Money is an issue for most directors, whether you work in a preschool or child development center. But for preschool directors, taking in enough tuition money for three hours of class to cover many of the same costs that full-day programs face is an additional challenge. Most preschools are non-profit organizations, so fundraising is a viable option to help raise money. There are many fundraising ideas and resources available. The following are a few ideas that have worked for other programs.

- Art show—Encourage the children to create art in vibrant colors using a variety of art media (drawing and coloring, sculpting, painting, and so on). Ask local framing stores to donate frames, mats, and other materials to display the artwork in an attractive manner. Invite the parents and other family members in for cookies and punch and let the bidding begin.
- Auction—This should be a night of fun. Consider hiring an auctioneer to come in and handle the bidding (the bids tend to be higher this way). I asked a director whose preschool held an annual auction what item brought in the highest bid. I was shocked at his answer—a carpool ticket. Although autographed baseballs, trips, oil paintings, and other valuable items were available, the most money was spent on a carpool ticket! The winner of the carpool ticket would be allowed to go to the front of the carpool line throughout the entire year. Apparently, time really was more important than money to that mom or dad. This particular school raised $25,000 in one evening without spending any money.
- Advertising— For a fee, offer advertising in your parent handbook, parent directory, and any other appropriate place. Photographers, children's doctors, dentists, and even hair salons usually advertise. Don't forget all of the extracurricular groups such as dancing, gymnastics, or boy scouts.
- Logo Supplies—Offering backpacks, juice cups, t-shirts, bibs, sweatshirts, and so on with the school logo is a great way to advertise for your school, provides parents with necessary materials, and earns extra money for your preschool.

Another way that many preschools save money is by not having a full kitchen in their programs. Because most children do not each lunch at preschool (or they bring their own lunches from home), it is not a necessity. However, this does make it extra challenging to offer nutritional snacks for children on a daily basis. Most of the preschool directors I talked to said parents take turns bringing in snacks for the children. I had a few questions for them: How do you monitor what they bring in? How do you know it is nutritional? How do you know the parent who prepared the snack used sanitary measures to protect the children? They shared a variety of answers, and the one I liked most was providing the parents with a snack guidelines handout (see Sample Snack Guidelines on page 207 in the Appendix). In addition to this, parents must be reminded of allergies and asked to follow policies and procedures regarding any food ban, such as peanuts, that you might have.

Parties

Parties take up a lot of time in a preschool. My advice is to keep them simple. Let the children make decorations for the party, and if possible, let them make the food, too. This cuts down on costs and, at the same time, increases the confidence and pride children have in their abilities.

Faith

Faith is an important part of most church preschools. Because church preschools are usually a ministry of the church, most churches would like faith-based lessons taught. Ask the appropriate church staff member(s) what expectations the church has. Clarify their expectations and express your approach to teaching faith with preschool children. What is your approach? It should be developmentally appropriate, which can be done using the basics. Sharing the fact that God loves each child, helping children understand right from wrong, and encouraging them to be kind to friends and family is probably enough for the preschool years. When sharing a Bible story, keep it simple and on the child's level. There is no need to get into deep theology regarding the story. Just tell it, and let the children ask questions. Work with the staff members, providing a list of basic faith songs that are appropriate for preschool children. Encourage staff members to model their faith with the children and each other. Be sensitive to staff members who might not be of the same faith. It is important that prospective staff members and parents know the church's and preschool's view on including faith in the classroom. It is respectful to share it with parents during their decision-making process.

Trust

Both the co-op director and the church director have unique working situations. The co-op director works for parents and the church director works for a pastor. I can imagine things can get confusing at times. The co-op director must balance being an employee of the parents and head of the program. Therefore, handling sensitive subjects may be difficult. Trust is really the key for you as a co-op preschool director. You must trust that when you inform the parents governing the preschool of certain situations that they will look at them objectively and act professionally. I suggest including the requirement that information remain confidential and that parents must act professionally despite their personal involvement as a parent.

Directors of church preschools have a different challenge. Some of you are staff members of the church and school and you have to balance your roles. Many times, children attend the church where they attend preschool and wires get crossed. For example, if a parent approaches you on Sunday about a preschool problem, simply let them know that you have on your Sunday "hat" and that you would love to talk to them on Monday. If it is something that cannot wait, go to a private place for the conversation.

The same applies to church staff. Encourage them to keep issues separate by discussing church issues during church staff meetings and preschool issues privately with you. If it doesn't stay separate, things can get confused. Confidentiality and trust are extremely important for you and the staff members on your team. Review your job descriptions for each job and make adjustments as necessary. When your job descriptions reflect your two separate jobs, use that to help you balance church and school.

Additional Resources for Preschool Directors

- Read *Preschool Director's Staff Development Handbook* by Kathleen Pullan Watkings and Lucias Durrant, Jr.
- Look up the article "Building a Healthy Preschool Director-Pastor Relationship" by Melvin M. Kieschnick at www.elca.org/lp/preschl.html.
- Contact the Parent Co-operative Preschool Co-operation at www.net/pcpc/index.html or by mail at 1571 Sandhurst Circle, PO Box 63512, Toronto, Ontario, Canada, M1V1V0.
- A great resource for church preschool directors is:
  www.lifeway.com/schoolresources/wee_committee.asp.
- A fun, interesting website for teachers, parents, and directors: www.edpysch.com.
- Read the article "The Keys to Success in Raising Funds" by Roger Neugebauer in the Sept/Oct 2001 issue of *Child Care Information Exchange.* www.childcareexchange.com.
- The May/June 2000 issue of *Child Care Information Exchange* has an article dedicated to church programs and another for co-op schools.
- Read "Way Beyond Bake Sales" by Anne Mitchell, The Parenting Exchange.
- Read the article "The Art of Fundraising" by Renne Targos in the November 2000 issue of *Child Care Business.*
- "Trading Control for Partnership" by Carol Gratsch Boyce is a helpful article for directors of co-operative preschools. Find it in the March 2002 issue of *Child Care Information Exchange.*
- Read "The Open-Door Policy: Enhancing Community in a Part-Time Preschool Program" by Todd Wanerman in the March 1999 issue of *Young Children.*

Appendix

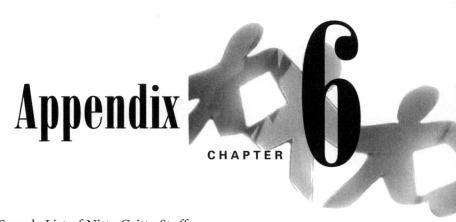

CHAPTER **6**

Sample List of Nitty Gritty Stuff

1. Band-aids can be found in each classroom in the "boo boo" box or in the office in the first aid kit.

2. The break room/resource room is located behind the school-age classrooms.

3. The soda machine is outside next to the playground.

4. Wipes, paper towels, and such are kept in the pantry of the kitchen.

5. Wendy's is the closest fast-food restaurant.

6. You don't have to use the children's bathroom; the adult bathroom is down the ramp to the left.

7. When you run out of accident reports or daily reports, check the cabinet marked FORMS in the office.

8. We keep a teacher's emergency kit in the office in the cabinet next to the one marked FORMS. In the kit you will find safety pins, cough drops, lotion, fingernail polish remover, needle and thread, and other personal items you might need.

9. The Mentor Teachers are Susan, Natalie, Kim, and Frankie. If an administrator can't be found and you have a question, ask one of them.

10. Your mailbox is located in the office above the time clock.

11. The number to the Pizza Hut that delivers to us is _____. The Chinese restaurant is _____.

12. The van keys are kept on a hook next to the copier in the office.

13. Film, batteries, and so on are kept in the drawer to the right of the time clock.

14. A center directory is in the drawer under the phone.

15. Time-off request forms can be found in the clear container next to the time clock.

Sample Scavenger Hunt

1. You need one box of tissues for your classroom. Please get it.

2. Your zipper broke. What do you need to repair it? Please get it.

3. Your mentor teacher needs a soda. Please get her one.

4. The director needs the number to Pizza Hut. What is it?

    _____

5. Show your mentor teacher where the bathroom is located.

6. You need more accident reports. Please go get them.

7. You have mail in your box. Go find it.

8. Ask a mentor teacher to sign this paper. (It can't be the one who is with you on this hunt.)

9. One of the toddler teachers is out of glue. Please get some from the resource room.

10. You need the director's cell phone number. Check the directory and write it here:

    _____

Staff Signature _____

Mentor Teacher Signature_____

Time _____

Sample Staff Questionnaire

Name _____

Classroom _____

I am looking forward to working with you at _____. Please take the time and share your thoughts with me (you can write your answers or just share them verbally with me). Thanks!

1. What is your favorite thing about your job?

_____

_____

_____

2. What is the one thing you most want me to know about you?

_____

_____

_____

3. What is the one thing you most want to know about me?

_____

_____

_____

4. What is your favorite age group to teach?

_____

_____

_____

5. If you are not currently teaching that age now, why not?

_____

_____

_____

6. Is there anything else you want to share with me?

_____

_____

_____

Sample Professional Development Training Plan

Areas of Potential Growth for Upcoming Year _____

Professional Goal for Upcoming Year _____

Topic	Training to Attend	Time Line

Director Signature _____ Date _____

Staff Signature _____ Date _____

Professional Development Survey

1. Why do you think you are a good teacher?

_____

_____

_____

2. What do you wish you did differently?

_____

_____

_____

3. When you attend training what topics do you tend to choose and why?

_____

_____

_____

4. What do you see yourself doing in:
1 year?

_____

_____

3 years?

_____

_____

5 years?

_____

_____

5. Do you prefer training on Saturday or a week night?

_____

Sample Mentor Job Qualifications

The Mentor Teacher position requires a minimum of a bachelor's degree in Child Development or related field and 2 years classroom experience, an associate's degree in Child Development or related field and 3 years of classroom experience, or a CDA credential and 5 years of classroom experience.

Sample Mentor Teacher Job Description (Additional Responsibilities)

1. Fulfill duties as a classroom teacher as stated in your job description.

2. Meet with age-group teachers once a month during staff meetings.

3. Participate in job interviews as the director sees necessary.

4. Assist in training new staff members, including but not limited to, role modeling, reviewing policy, assisting with scavenger hunt, and answering questions.

5. Facilitate center tours in the absence of an administrator upon request of the director.

6. Dispense medicine to necessary children as scheduled on medicine log in the absence of an administrator or upon request of the director.

7. Attend an additional 6 hours of training per year on administrative/ leadership topics.

8. Facilitate at least one 10-minute training per year at a staff meeting based on new information learned in a leadership workshop.

Sample Mentor Teacher Application

Name _____

1. What is your vision of a mentor teacher?

_____

_____

_____

_____

2. Why do you desire to be a mentor teacher?

_____

_____

_____

_____

3. What strengths do you possess that will assist you in your role as a mentor teacher, if hired?

_____

_____

_____

_____

4. What challenges do you anticipate, if any, in taking on the role of mentor teacher?

_____

_____

_____

5. Have you read the job qualifications and responsibilities for the position? Do you have any questions? If so, please explain.

_____

_____

_____

Sample Staff Meeting Schedule

Monthly topic: Communication

6:30 - Dinner (welcome new staff, sing "Happy Birthday" to those celebrating a birthday that month)

6:50 - Pass the Clap*

7:00 - Communication (Elements of Communication and Active Listening exercise, set communication goal for the month)

7:20 - Open the floor for issues staff want to address

7:30 - Age-group meetings

8:00 - Staff Committees

8:30 - Dismiss

*Pass the Clap is a great communication exercise. Have all staff members stand in a circle, including the director. The director will "pass the clap" to the person on the right by turning and facing that person and trying to clap at the same time. That person will then turn to the next person and "pass the clap." The clap will continue to be passed until it is back to you. At that point you explain to the participants that the clap might be passed at the same time if you look at each other's eyes instead of each other's hands. The clap is passed around the circle again and usually a nice rhythm is developed. Try adding a second clap going the other way and even a third group of clapping all at the same time. Chaos soon takes over. Communication is similar. When we are focused and ready to communicate we can be prepared and it makes sense. But once we have many things coming at us at once—for example, parents, children, and other staff—communication breaks down and turns into chaos. Try it at your next staff meeting!

Sample Yearly Staff Questionnaire

Thank you for taking time to complete this questionnaire. I appreciate your honest opinions. We will be discussing the results at next month's staff meeting. Please feel free to write or type your answers.

1. How would you describe this past year as a staff member?

2. What was your favorite part about working as a team member this past year?

3. What was your least favorite part?

4. What suggestions do you have to make the above situation better?

5. Do you feel valued as a staff member in our program? Why?

6. What else would you like me to know about last year or this upcoming year?

Additional comments:

Sample Yearly Staff Evaluation

Staff Member _____ Date _____

Classroom Management	Strongly Agree	Agree	Strongly Disagree	Disagree	Additional Comments:
Classroom environment is inviting and arranged to meet the developmental needs of the classroom.					
Daily schedule is flexible and represents the needs of the children.					
Lesson plan consists of appropriate activities and represents the needs of the children in the classroom.					
Is prepared for day.					
Facilitates activities that promote growth in all areas of development.					
Develops goals for each child based on observations.					
Is flexible and responds to the needs of the children in the classroom.					
Is an appropriate role model in the classroom.					
Uses appropriate guidance techniques with children.					
Transitions between activities in an appropriate, effective manner.					
Maintains a clean and safe environment.					

Interaction With Children	Strongly Agree	Agree	Strongly Disagree	Disagree	Additional Comments:
Greets children by name.					
Responds to children's questions.					
Uses a calm voice when speaking with children.					
Speaks with children at their eye level.					
Shares affection with children.					
Uses positive guidance techniques.					
Shows respect for each child's uniqueness.					
Acknowledges children's accomplishments.					
Avoids and discourages labeling or stereotyping.					
Interaction With Parents					
Greets parents by first name.					
Responds to parents' questions and concerns in an appropriate time manner					
Keeps parents informed about their child's day.					
Keeps parents informed about upcoming events.					
Facilitates parent conferences twice a year and as needed.					

	Strongly Agree	Agree	Strongly Disagree	Disagree	Additional Comments:
Is professional when dealing with parents.					
Is available and approachable by all parents.					
Encourages parent involvement in the classroom.					
Shows respect for parents as the authority for the child.					
Maintains confidentiality.					
Interaction With Team Members					
Works well with co-teacher.					
Is approachable by new team members.					
Does not gossip.					
Shares materials and information readily.					
Is a team player.					
Accepts constructive criticism.					
Is willing to help out when needed.					

Professionalism, Work Habits, and Continued Education	Strongly Agree	Agree	Strongly Disagree	Disagree	Additional Comments:
Is courteous to prospective staff and parents.					
Is ethical.					
Arrives at work on time.					
Has an acceptable attendance record.					
Follows sick and vacation policy when requesting time off.					
Has a positive outlook throughout the day.					
Is flexible.					
Maintains confidentiality regarding center information.					
Meets annual requirement for continued education.					
Seeks out additional continued educational opportunities.					
Meets Training Plan from previous year.					
Applies new information gained in training.					
Is willing to share new information with other team members.					

Sample Yearly Parent Survey

Dear Parents,

Thank you for taking time to complete this annual survey. We value your opinions regarding the care of your child, and we welcome any suggestions you have for making it better. If you would like to set up an appointment with me to further discuss any of the questions or your comments on this survey, please stop by my office to do so.

I will be posting a summary of this survey in our parent newsletter next month.

With your child in mind,

_____, Director

1. Describe the past year in our program from your perspective:

2. Describe the past year in our program from your child's perspective:

3. How would you describe the program when you enter the center in the morning?

4. Are you and your child greeted in the morning when you arrive? If so, how? And by whom?

5. Are you and your child told goodbye upon your departure? If so, how? And by whom?

6. What is one word you would use when describing our program to a friend?

7. What is something that you appreciate about our program?

8. What would you like to see added or changed in our program? Why?

Additional Comments:

Sample Developmental Checklists: Infant, Toddler, and Preschool

Name _____ Date of Birth _____

0-14 months

Developmental Milestone	Date Observed	Staff Initials
Gross Motor		
____ Lifts head	_____	_____
____ Rolls from stomach to back	_____	_____
____ When pulled to sit, head is steady	_____	_____
____ Able to lift shoulders off mat while on stomach	_____	_____
____ Sits with support	_____	_____
____ Rolls from back to stomach	_____	_____
____ Sits without support	_____	_____
____ Creeps or crawls	_____	_____
____ Pulls self to stand	_____	_____
____ Stands alone	_____	_____
____ Cruises while holding onto furniture	_____	_____
____ Walks with assistance	_____	_____
____ Begins to creep up stairs	_____	_____
____ Squats to recover toy (might fall)	_____	_____
____ Walks well (may not occur by 14 months)	_____	_____
Fine Motor		
____ Reaches for objects	_____	_____
____ Grasps objects (with 2 hands)	_____	_____
____ Places objects in mouth	_____	_____
____ Transfers objects between hands	_____	_____
____ Bangs toys in play	_____	_____
____ Drops toys in play	_____	_____
____ Reaches for toys dropped	_____	_____
____ Holds cup (with 2 hands)	_____	_____
____ Uses pincer grasp (thumb and index finger)	_____	_____
____ Begins to feed self	_____	_____

Language

____ Turns head according to noises

____ Coos

____ Laughs aloud

____ Babbles

____ Attempts to imitate sounds

____ Understands *no*

____ Says "ma ma" or "da da"

____ Says 1-3 words

Cognitive

____ Eyes follow moving objects

____ Looks at objects in hand

____ Responds to facial expressions

____ Responds to simple directions

____ Places objects in containers, then takes them out

____ Recognizes people

Social Emotional

____ Has a spontaneous social smile

____ Enjoys play

____ Recognizes parents and main caregiver

____ Discriminates strangers

____ Recognizes names

____ Enjoys looking at self in mirror

____ Enoys peek-a-boo

____ Shows emotions (happy, sad, angry)

____ Waves bye-bye

____ Plays alone

14-36 months

Developmental Milestone	Date Observed	Staff Initials

Gross Motor

____ Walks alone

____ Recovers toys from floor without falling

____ Pulls a pull toy while walking

____ Climbs stairs

____ Closes doors

____ Seats self on chair

____ Attempts to walk backwards

____ Climbs down stairs

_____ Moves body to music

_____ Kicks ball

_____ Jumps with both feet

_____ Bends at waist to retrieve objects

_____ Stands on one foot with hand held

_____ Walks on tiptoes

_____ Balances on one foot for a second or two

Fine Motor

_____ Stacks 2-4 blocks

_____ Places rings on a stick

_____ Turns pages of a book (3 or 4 at a time)

_____ Uses spoon

_____ Drinks from only a cup

_____ Scribbles with large crayons

_____ Removes shoes and socks

_____ Unzips large zipper

_____ Opens doors

_____ Turns pages of a book (1 at a time)

_____ Strings 4 large beads

_____ Takes off coat

_____ Washes and dries hands

_____ Puts on coat

_____ Attempts to draw circles and straight lines

_____ Pours from small pitcher

Language

_____ Points to objects when asked

_____ Points to one or more body parts

_____ Understands prepositions such as *on*, *in*, and *under*

_____ Follows one-part directions

_____ Says own name

_____ Says "mine" and "no"

_____ Has a vocabulary of about 50 words

_____ Answers some basic questions

_____ Points to common objects in pictures

_____ Understands *no*, *don't*, and *can't*

_____ Knows simples rhymes and songs

_____ Asks what, where, and why questions

_____ Shows frustration when not understood

_____ Uses plurals

_____ Has a vocabulary of about 100-300 words

Cognitive

_____ Imitates actions and words of adults   _____   _____

_____ Looks at pictures in a book   _____   _____

_____ Follows two-part directions   _____   _____

_____ Matches two similar objects   _____   _____

_____ Stacks rings on peg in order of size   _____   _____

_____ Recognizes self in mirror   _____   _____

_____ Imitates adults behaviors   _____   _____

_____ Recognizes simple shapes   _____   _____

_____ Anticipates the need to urinate or defecate   _____   _____

Social Emotional

_____ Responds to "no" by peers or adults   _____   _____

_____ Refers to self by name   _____   _____

_____ Plays side by side other children   _____   _____

_____ Believes all toys are his/her own   _____   _____

_____ Observes other children playing together   _____   _____

_____ Participates in simple group games & activities   _____   _____

_____ Knows own sex   _____   _____

3- to 5-year-olds

Developmental Milestone	Date Observed	Staff Initials

Gross Motor

_____ Stands on one foot for 3-5 seconds   _____   _____

_____ Walks up stairs alternating feet   _____   _____

_____ Throws ball overhand   _____   _____

_____ Broad jumps   _____   _____

_____ Pumps self on swing   _____   _____

_____ Walks backwards toes to heels   _____   _____

_____ Skips   _____   _____

Fine Motor

_____ Uses scissors   _____   _____

_____ Copies a circle, line, and cross   _____   _____

_____ Zips zippers and buttons buttons   _____   _____

_____ Draws person with at least 2 body parts   _____   _____

_____ Attempts to write own name   _____   _____

_____ Dresses self after toileting   _____   _____

_____ Cuts on a line   _____   _____

____ Serves self at snack and meals

____ Cleans up after self at meals

____ Cuts easy foods with knife

____ Laces shoes

Language

____ Identifies more than five body parts

____ Asks questions

____ Has a vocabulary of 500 words or more

____ Counts to 12

____ Follows three-part directions

____ Tells stories

____ Joins sentences together

____ Asks when, how, and why questions

____ Has a vocabulary of 1000 words or more

____ Repeats simple story, but may confuse facts

Cognitive

____ Builds 8-10 block towers

____ Matches colors

____ Knows full name

____ Repeats 3 digits

____ Expresses 4 primary colors properly

____ Begins rhyming words

____ Makes up words

____ Matches pictures of similar objects

____ Identifies a few letters in the alphabet

____ Talks about yesterday, today, and tomorrow

____ Identifies address (street and town)

Social Emotional

____ Identifies own sex

____ Begins playing cooperatively with others

____ Separates from parents easily

____ Enjoys playing make believe and dramatic play

____ Enjoys dramatic play with "babies"

____ Is able to take turns

____ Enjoys making jokes and exaggeration

____ Able to problem solve simple situations

____ Shares fear in conversation and dialogue

____ Is able to identify and communicate feelings

Sample Special Needs Policy

_____ (Name of center) _____ will make every effort to meet the needs of your child physically, emotionally, intellectually, and socially within our abilities based on our staffing, ratio, and facility resources. We will work with families in making necessary plans to accommodate your child in our program as long as necessary. We look forward to working with you at every stage of your child's development to ensure a warm, secure environment for your child to grow and learn.

Sample Sick Policy

It is the goal of _____ (Name of center) _____ to provide a safe and healthy environment for your child. In an ideal world we could accomplish this in a germ-free environment. However, germs are spread every day when two children's worlds collide in our facility. Even though we pride ourselves in adhering to proper hand washing and sanitizing procedures, germs are still spread. With the help of parents keeping their sick children at home, we can help prevent the spread of even more germs and illnesses in our center.

When is your child too sick to attend school? When they are displaying one of the following symptoms:

- Fever
- Diarrhea
- Vomiting
- Undiagnosed rash
- Red eyes with discharge
- Nose with colored discharge that requires constant wiping
- Headache that will not respond to ibuprofen or acetaminophen
- Cannot participate in the daily activities of the program

If your child develops any of these symptoms at school, you will be contacted and asked to pick up your child immediately. If you cannot be reached within one hour, we will call one of your approved contacts.

Your child may return to school when he or she is symptom-free for at least 24 hours or has been on antibiotics for the appropriate time as determined by your child's pediatrician. If your child has been seen by a doctor and is told he or she may return to school sooner than 24 hours, please provide a note from the doctor. Upon your child's arrival, the director or your child's teacher will conduct a health check to ensure the child is free of fever and any other obvious symptom.

Remember, proper hand washing at home helps prevent the spread of germs. Wash your hands and the hands of your child often.

Essential Books for Parent Library

101 Easy, Wacky, Crazy Activities for Young Children by Carole Dibble and Kathy Lee (Gryphon House, 2000).

101 Great Gifts from Kids by Stephanie Mueller and Ann Wheeler (Gryphon House, 2002).

125 Brain Games for Toddlers and Twos by Jackie Silberg (Gryphon House, 2000).

Around the Family Table by Ronda Coleman (Robins Lane Press, 2001).

Baby Signs by Linda Acredolo, PhD and Susan Goodwyn, PhD (McGraw-Hill/Contemporary Books, 2002).

Before the Basics by Bev Bos (Turn the Page Press, 1983).

The Business Traveling Parent by Dan Verdick (Robins Lane Press, 2000).

The Five Love Languages of Children by Gary D. Chapman (Northfield Publishing, 1997).

Games to Play with Babies by Jackie Silberg (Gryphon House, 2001).

Games to Play with Two-Year-Olds by Jackie Silberg (Gryphon House, 2002).

The Gesell Institute's Child From One to Six by Louis B. Ames (Harper Row, 1989).

The Gift of Play: And Why Your Child Cannot Thrive Without It by M.W. Piers and G.M. Landau (Walker & Co., 1980).

Help! There's a Toddler in My House! by Nancy Kelly (Robins Lane Press, 2001).

Honey for a Child's Heart by Gladys M. Hunt (Zondervan, 2002).

The Hurried Child by David Elkind (Perseus Publishing, 2001).

Miseducation by David Elkind (Knopf, 1998).

Mister Rogers Parenting Book: Helping to Understand Your Young Child by Fred Rogers (Running Press, 2002).

More Than the ABCs by Judith A. Schickedanz (National Association for the Education of Young Children, 1986).

On Becoming a Family by T. Berry Brazelton (Delta Trade Paperbacks, 1982).

Parent's Guide to Early Childhood Education by Diane Trister Dodge (Teaching Strategies, 1995).

Parenting After Divorce by Philip Michael Stahl (Impact Publishers, Inc., 2000).

Preschool for Parents by Diane Trister Dodge (Sourcebooks Trade, 1998).

The Preschool Years: Family Strategies That Work—From Experts and Parents by Ellen Gallinsky (Ballantine Books, 1991).

Raising Your Spirited Child by Mary Sheedy Kurcinka (Perennial, 1992).

Sign With Your Baby by Joseph Garcia (Northlight Communications, 1999).

Talking With Young Children About Adoption by Mary Watkins and Susan Fisher (Yale University Press, 1995).

Tell Me Again About the Night I Was Born by Jamie Lee Curtis (HarperCollins Juvenile Books, 1996).

The Wonder of Boys by Michael Gurian (J.P. Tarcher, 1997).

Sample Policy Concerning Dispensing Medicine

Only medicine prescribed by a physician will be dispensed in our center. It must be properly signed in and then locked in the appropriate storage area. All medication must be in its original container with the child's full name and dosage written on it. The center will provide disposable medicine cups for dispensing medications, so it is not necessary to include cups or syringes.

A member of the office staff or another designated staff member will dispense the medicine twice daily, at 11:00 a.m. and 3:00 p.m. Medicine that is to be given only twice a day will not be dispensed twice at the center. Therefore, please choose a time at home to dispense the medicine and another time (11 or 3) at the center.

All medicine must be properly signed in on the medication form in order to be dispensed. Failure to properly sign in medicine will force the office staff NOT to dispense medicine to your child. Please write your child's name, prescription name and number, dosage, time to be given, and your signature on the medication form each day.

Please take home all medicines at the end of each day.

Medicine Authorization Form

Date _____

Parents,
Please complete the entire form in order to ensure your child's medicine is properly dispensed. Please make sure that the medicine is secured in the locked box/refrigerator provided. All medicine must be in its original container, and labeled with the child's full name.

Child's Name			
Medicine Name			
Prescription #			
Amount Needs			
Refrigeration?	Yes or No	Yes or No	Yes or No
Time (circle one)	11AM or 3PM	11AM or 3PM	11AM or 3PM
Parent's Signature			
For Office Use Only			
Adverse Reactions			
Staff Initials			

Accident/Injury Report

Child's Name _____

Time and Date of Accident _____

Describe Accident (What were the circumstances surrounding this accident?):

_____

_____

_____

Describe Injury (What part of the body was injured?):

_____

_____

_____

Describe First Aid Procedures (How was the injury cared for?):

_____

_____

Staff Present at Time of Accident

_____

Was professional medical attention necessary? **Yes No** (If yes, answer the following questions)
Name, Address, and Phone Number of Medical Facility That Treated the Child

_____

Name of Medical Personnel who Treated the Child

_____

Was DHR contacted within 24 hours? **Yes No** By Whom? _____ Time/Date _____

Staff Completing Accident Report _____

Administrative Signature_____

Staff Notifying Parent _____ Time _____

Parent Signature _____

Every Family Is Different

Following is a list of helpful resources about divorce.

Websites:
http://pbskids.org/rogers/parents/parentdivorce.html
http://www.hec.ohio-state.edu/famlife/divorce/pguides/intro.htm
http://www.uky.edu/PR/NewsFeatures/NF-divorce.html
http://www.divorcesource.com/MD/ARTICLES/berndt1.html
http://www.cbsnews.com/stories/2002/02/01/earlyshow/saturday/main327911.shtml
http://www.childcare.ws/articles.htm

Books for Children:

The Chimpanzee Kid by Ron Roy (Clarion, 1985). After his parents divorce, Harold gets involved in a rescue adventure. (Grades 5–6)

Dinosaurs Divorce: A Guide for Changing Families by Laurene and Marc Brown (Boston Little Brown and Co, 1986). Confounded young children are helped by a family of dinosaurs. (Age 3-7)

Divorce is a Grownup Problem by Janet Sinberg (Avon, 1978). This book explains divorce; good for parents to read with the child. Contains a bibliography of other books on divorce. (Age 3-7)

Don't Make Me Smile by Barbara Park (Knopf, 1981). A humorous and empathetic story of divorce from a child's point of view. (Grades 4–5)

It's Not Your Fault, Koko Bear by Vicky Lansky (Book Peddlers, 1998). Koko is reassured that his parents' divorce is not his fault and that they still love him. (Age 3-7)

Let's Talk About Divorce by Fred Rogers (Putnam, 1996). Contains photographs and easy-to-understand text. (Age 3-7)

A Look at Divorce by Margaret Sanford Pursell; photos by Maria S. Forrai (Lerner Publications, 1977). Reassures children that even though parents divorce, the child is still loved. (Age 3-7)

Mama and Daddy Bear's Divorce by Cornelia Spelman (Albert Whitman, 1998). (Age 3-7)

My Family's Changing by Pat Thomas (Barron's Education Series, 1999). Divorce is explained in simple language. (Age 3-8)

Stepchild by Terry Berger (Julian Messner, 1980). This book is about adjusting to a step-parent. (Age 5-10)

Two Places to Sleep by Joan Schuchman (Carol Rhoda Books, 1979). A father is awarded custody of the children. (Age 4-7)

Books for Teachers and Parents:

Growing Up With a Single Parent by Sara Mclanahan and Gary Sandefur (Harvard University Press, 1994).

Second Chances by Judith S. Wallerstein and Sandra Blakeslee (Ticknor & Fields, 1990).

Magazine Articles for Teachers and Parents:

"The Negative Messages That Even Good Parents Send" by Ron Taffel, Ph. D in the May 1, 2002 issue of *Parents Magazine*.

"Children of Divorce" by Dr. Adele Brodkin and her colleague, Melba Coleman, Ed.D in the Jan/Feb 1995 issue of *Instructor*.

Sample Visitor Card

Parent Name _____

Parent Address _____

_____

Employer _____

     Phone Number _____

     Work Number _____

     Cell Phone Number _____

Parent Name _____

Parent Address _____

_____

Employer _____

     Phone Number _____

     Work Number _____

     Cell Phone Number _____

Child's Name _____ DOB (or due date) _____

Child's Name _____ DOB (or due date) _____

Child's Name _____ DOB (or due date) _____

Anticipated Enrollment Date _____ Anticipated classroom(s) _____

For Office Only

Date/Time of Tour _____

Tour Guide _____

Notes:

Components of a Parent Handbook

Welcome

Introduction
History and Mission of Program
Philosophy
Mission Statement
Non-Discriminatory Policy
Special Needs Policy

Operational Information
Address
Phone and Fax Numbers
Website/E-mail
Tax ID Number
Operating Hours
Holidays
School Closings (e.g., inclement
   weather)

Enrollment Information
Tour
Enrollment Procedures
   Transition
Your Child's First Day at School
   What to Wear
   What to Bring
Parent Visits and Phone Calls
Arrivals and Departures
Release of Children
Withdrawal

Health and Nutrition
Required Immunizations

Sick Policy
Daily Health Screening

Tuition Information
Registration Fee
Payment Policy
Multi-Child Discount
Absences
Late Fees
Late Pick-Up
Field Trips

Dispensing of Medicine
Meals and Snacks
Emergency Procedures
Security
Accidents

Classroom Information
Teacher Qualifications
Ratios
Curriculum
Guidance Approach
Pets
Visitors
Field Trips
Birthdays
Storage
Toilet Training

Parent Information
Parent Involvement
Parent Library
Newsletters
Parent Conferences

Sample Philosophy Regarding Early Childhood Education

It is the philosophy of _____ (Name of center) _____ that children are unique individuals who deserve a warm, secure environment that promotes a sense of wonder and discovery in learning. We encourage children to develop socially, intellectually, and creatively as they grow. We value an inclusive environment that respects the distinctive qualities of others and individual aspect of themselves. We partner with parents to promote and enhance the child's growth and development.

Sample Ice Breakers for Parents and Staff

Pass the Clap

Pass the Clap is a great communication exercise. Have all the staff members stand in a circle, including the director. The director will "pass the clap" to the person on his or her right by turning and facing that person and trying to clap at the same time. That person will then turn to the next person and "pass the clap." The clap will continue to be passed until it is back to the director. At this point, explain to the participants that the clap is to be passed at the same time if you look at each other's eyes instead of each other's hands. The clap is passed around the circle again and usually a nice rhythm is developed. Try adding a second clap going the other way, and even a third group of clapping all at the same time. Chaos soon takes over. Communication is similar to this. When we are focused and ready to communicate, we can be prepared and it makes sense. But once we have many things coming at us at once (such as parents, children, and other staff), communication quickly breaks down and turns into chaos.

Phonics Name Game

This is a great activity for any group, even school-age children. Ask the group to form a circle. Stand in the middle and show the group a ball (an unusual ball is fun). Toss the ball to someone in the circle and introduce yourself with a phonetic description; for example, I am usually "Crazy Kathy." The ball continues to be tossed until everyone in the group has had a turn. Following the same pattern, toss the ball again. The third time, things change. Instead of saying your own name when you toss the ball, you must say the name (and phonetic description) of the person you are tossing to. This is fun game, and you will learn a few names that will be hard to forget.

The Key to Knowing Me

Most adults have keys of some sort with them during meetings. Form groups of 4-6 participants and ask them to take out their keys. Using their keys, the participants tell about themselves. It is a quick and easy way to break the ice. I always have my keys available in case someone doesn't have a set (it is fun to see what they say about my keys).

My Favorite Place to Shop

This is a great activity when you are addressing room arrangement. Think about the most common stores in a mall and write each one down on a separate piece of large paper (I love to use those 3M large Post it Pads). I usually write down a department store, candy store, lingerie store, shoe store, toy store, candle store, and clothing store. Place signs around the room, providing enough space for a group to gather. Invite participants to find the store of their choice and go to it. Have the group designate someone to write down the answers to the following questions on the large sheet of paper:

> Why do you like this store?
> What do you notice when you enter this store?
> What makes you want to stay and shop?
> Compare the lists from each store. Notice the similarities and differences. Most can be applied to the classroom. Not all children like it loud or bright; some like warm, quiet spaces; and others might like music. I love this one!

What Do We Have in Common?

This is a super team builder. I remember some African-American teachers commenting I must have more in common with a Russian staff member because we both had the same skin color. By participating in this activity, however, they discovered that we grew up in very similar homes and liked almost exactly the same foods. Divide your staff into teams of four people. Explain that each team must come up with three unique things they have in common. Next, two teams of four join together and repeat the activity, but must come up with three more new things. Teams continue to join until the group becomes one. It will become a little more challenging coming up with three unique things with one group. It might take a few minutes, but it can be done!

Sample Parent Involvement Survey

We would like your input on the future involvement of parents in our program. Please take the time to complete this survey and give us your input. Results of this survey will be noted in next month's parent newsletter.

Thank you!

1. Would you like to see more parent involvement in our program?

_____ yes   _____ no

2. Would you be willing to participate on a parent committee?

_____ yes   _____ no

3. If yes, which parent committee would you be willing to serve on?

___ Teacher Appreciation   ___ Special Events   ___ Facility and Grounds

___ Welcoming   ___ Memory   ___ Fellowship

4. Would you be willing to chair or co-chair a committee?

_____ yes   ___ no

Name _____

Phone _____ E-mail _____

Sample Community Survey

Dear Parents,

We understand that a good part of your day is spent getting your child to and from school and getting yourself to and from work. As we state in our philosophy, we believe that we are partners with you on this journey, so we would like to help. What can we do to better serve you? (Results will be posted in next month's newsletter.)

1. Are there any events, trainings, seminars, and so on that you would like to see our center include?

_____

_____

2. Are there any services (e.g., family photos) we could consider hosting to make your life easier?

_____

_____

3. What is your biggest stress regarding time?

_____

_____

4. Is there anything we offer in our program that we consider helpful, but you do not?

_____

_____

5. If so, how would like to see it changed?

_____

_____

6. Additional comments:

_____

_____

Sample Child Development Handout for Parents' Night Out

Quotes and Sayings to Remember:
- "Imagination is more important than knowledge." Albert Einstein
- Think process, not product, when it comes to art.
- The child is the curriculum.
- Honor what is natural.
- Learning involves feelings!

Books to Check Out:

Before the Basics by Bev Bos

Building Your Baby's Brain: A Parent's Guide to the First Five Years by Diane Trister Dodge and Cate Heroman

By the Ages: Behavior and Development of Children Pre-Birth through Eight by K. Eileen Allen and Lynn R. Marotz

The Gift of Play: And Why Your Child Cannot Thrive Without It by M.W. Piers and G.M. Landau

Miseducation and the Hurried Child by David Elkind

Preschool for Parents: What Every Parent Needs to Know About Preschool by Diane Trister Dodge and Toni S. Bickart

Rethinking the Brain: New Insights into Early Development by Rima Shore

The Trouble With Perfect: How to Avoid the Overachievement Trap and Still Raise Successful Children by Elisabeth Guthrie and Kathy Matthews

Websites on Child Development:

www.naeyc.org
www.earlychildhood.com
www.scholastic.com
www.ghbooks.com
www.familyeducation.com

A good journal to read is *Young Children* by the National Association for the Education of Young Children (NAEYC). It is available through NAEYC membership, and by subscription at $15/yr. A bi-monthly journal, it features articles on theory, practice, and research; professional and children's book reviews; public policy; and viewpoints on current issues.

Sample Daily Schedule

Monday

6:45 AM	Arrive, check messages, turn on lights, unlock doors, write information for day on staff communication board, turn on computer and copier
7:15 –8:00	Center opens at 7:15 AM, greet children (wearing headset for phone), walk through halls checking on teachers
8:30	Scheduled parent meeting to discuss behavior situation in preschool room
9:00	Review calendar for week
9:30	Classroom observation in infant room
10:00	Check messages, return phone calls
10:30	Check e-mail, look up a few articles for upcoming toddler parent meeting
11:00	Dispense medicine
11:30	Check on and help out with lunch if needed
12:00 Noon	Review classroom observation from morning
12:30	Meet with infant teachers to discuss transition ideas and observation
1:00	Lunch
2:00	Open, sort, and answer mail
2:30	Check on and deliver afternoon snack
3:00	Dispense medicine
3:30	Prospective parent tour (I usually schedule 1 hour for tours)
4:00	" "
4:30	Check messages, return phone calls
5:00	Tidy office for tomorrow
5:30	Head home (if there are no emergencies) after saying good-bye to staff and children
6:00	Assistant director or lead staff member in charge of closing center
6:30	Center closes
7:00 PM	Lights off

Sample "To Go" Snack Survey

Dear Parents,

We are considering adding a "to go" snack in the evenings for your children to eat on the way home. We would like to know if this is something that you are interested in before we consider it further. Please complete the survey and give it to your child's teacher.

Thank you!

1. Are you interested in adding a "to go" snack in the evenings?

   _____ yes   _____ no

(If no, you can turn in your survey at this point.)

2. Are you willing to add $1.00 to your weekly tuition to cover this expense?

   _____ yes   _____ no

3. Are you willing to bring in occasional snacks to help defray costs of "to go" snacks (in lieu of the $1.00 tuition increase)?

   _____ yes   _____ no

4. What type of snacks would you like to see offered?

   Cheerios _____   Trail Mix _____   Goldfish _____   Pretzels _____
   Animal Crackers _____   Other (please describe) _____

Additional comments or questions:

_____

_____

_____

_____

_____

Sample Field Trip Checklist

Date of Field Trip _____

Field Trip Destination _____

Address _____

Phone Number _____

Contact Name _____

Class Name _____

Teacher(s) Attending _____

_____

Other Adults Attending _____

_____

TRANSPORTATION

Departure:
Gas Amount   ¼   ½   ¾   full

Van Condition
Poor   Fair   Clean

Mileage _____

Return:
Gas Amount   ¼   ½   ¾   full

Van Condition
Poor   Fair   Clean

Mileage _____

Driver's signature

_____

Child's Name	On Van	At Site	During Site	On Van	In Classroom
1.					
2.					
3.					
4.					
5.					
6.					
7.					
8.					
9.					
10.					
11.					
12.					

Staff Member Completing This Form_____

Sample Snack Guidelines

We would like you to follow these snack guidelines when planning your snack for your child's preschool classroom. Thank you for assisting us in offering quality nutrition for your children.

- **Water** is the drink of choice. It is not necessary to bring juice with your snack.
- When planning snacks, please take time to choose foods that are **healthy** for the children. **Fruits, vegetables, and whole grain breads and cereals** make a great choice. It is okay to add small amounts of lean meats and dairy. We ask that you not bring in snacks that are high in sugar such as donuts, cookies, and so on. We will save these kinds of treats for special occasions.

Choose from the following snack suggestions or create your own ideas with your child:

- Cut up fresh, raw fruits and vegetables. Providing a dip can spice things up.
- Homemade granola is a favorite. Start with rolled oats and add things such as dried fruits, sesame seeds and coconut. Please do not add nuts due to a high number of peanut allergies. Melt butter and honey, stir, and pour over granola mixture. Bake at 350 degrees for 10 minutes, stir, and bake another 5 minutes. Granola can be served alone, with yogurt, or with milk.
- Mini sandwiches offer great snacks for children. Try using mini pita bread, or cut wheat bread into interesting shapes using cookie cutters.
- Smoothies can be made in a variety of ways and are a nice change.
- Tortilla crisps are yummy. Start with whole-wheat tortillas. Melt butter and spread a small amount over the tortilla, sprinkle cinnamon and sugar on top, and bake at 350 degrees for 5 minutes. Cut into triangles and serve.
- Tortilla roll-ups are also a favorite. Spread cream cheese on a tortilla. Add shredded carrots, pineapple, and raisins. Roll it up, slice, and serve.

Thank you for helping us help your children.

Bibliography

Challenges Related to Staff

Articles

Alexander, N. Nov/Dec 1999. Understanding Adults as Learners. *Child Care Information Exchange*, 130, 82-84.

Bruno, H.E., & M. Leitch Copeland. Mar/Apr 2001. Countering Center Gossip. *Child Care Information Exchange*, 138, 22-26.

Bulion, L. 2002. Ways to Celebrate Teacher Appreciation Week. *Education World.* <www.education-world.com/a_admin/admin162.shtml> (27 February, 2003).

Cannata Heng, A. Sept/Oct 2001. Hiring the Right Person. *Child Care Information Exchange*, 141, 10-12.

Carter, M. Ideas for Training Staff. Continuing monthly column. *Child Care Information Exchange.*

Carter, M. Sept/Oct 2001. Right From the Start: Changing Our Approach to Staff Orientation. *Child Care Information Exchange*, 141, 79-81.

Ensman, R. April 1996. "Are You an Active Listener?" IS Magazine <www.isdesignet.com/magazine/apr'96/commentary.html> (15 april, 2003).

Forrest, R., & N. McCrea. Jan/Feb 2002. How Do I Relate and Share Professionally? *Child Care Information Exchange*, 143, 49-52.

Genishi, C., & A. Jul/Aug 1996. Haas Dyson. Ways of Talking: Respecting Differences. *Child Care Information Exchange*, 110, 43-46.

Hudson, S.J. Spring 2000. "So you had a good day?" Educators Learn via E-mail. *Dimensions of Early Childhood*, 28 (2), 17-21.

Olsen, G.W. & S.W. Shirley. Sept/Oct 2001. Resolving Staff Conflict. *Child Care Information Exchange*, 141, 22-24.

Petty, K. Summer 1999. Who's Caring for Caregivers? *Texas Child Care Quarterly* 23(1).

Smith, C.J. May/June 1999. Ongoing Growing—Overcoming Obstacles to Training Staff. *Child Care Information Exchange*, 127, 9-11.

Preserving Memories: A Blueprint for Teachers. Spring 2000. *Dimensions of Early Childhood*, 28 (2), 22-27.

Steelsmith, S. Aug 16, 1997. Encouraging Preschoolers to Share. Adaptation of *I Want It* by E. Crary. 1986. Seattle, WA: Parenting Press. <http://www.parentingpress.com/t_970816.html> (27 February, 2003).

Steelsmith, S. Aug 30, 1997. Learning How to Take Turns. Adaptation of *I Can't Wait* by E. Crary. 1986. Seattle, WA: Parenting Press. <www.parentingpress.com/t_970830.html> (27 February, 2003).

Books

Alexander, N. 2000. *Early Childhood Workshops That Work!: The Essential Guide to Successful Training and Workshops.* Beltsville, MD: Gryphon House, Inc.

Carter Dyke, P., & P. Schiller. 2001. *The Practical Guide to Quality Child Care.* Beltsville, MD: Gryphon House, Inc.

Carter, M. & D. Curtis. 1995. *Training Teachers: A Harvest of Theory and Practice.* Saint Paul, MN: Redleaf Press.

Engel, B., & G. Gronlund. 2001. *Focused Portfolios: A Complete Assessment for the Young Child.* Saint Paul, MN: Redleaf Press.

Grace, C., & E. Shores. 1998. *The Portfolio Book: A Step-By-Step Guide for Teachers.* Beltsville, MD: Gryphon House, Inc.

Illsley Clark, J. 1998. *Who, Me Lead a Group?* Seattle, WA: Parenting Press.

Jones, E. (editor). 1993. *Growing Teachers: Partnerships in Staff Development.* Washington, DC: NAEYC.

Jorde Bloom, P. 2000. *The Circle of Influence: Implementing Shared Decision Making and Participative Management.* Lake Forest, IL: New Horizons.

Jorde Bloom. P. 2002. *Making the Most of Meetings: a Practical Guide.* Lake Forest, IL: New Horizons.

Mueller, S., & A. Wheeler. 2002. *101 Great Gifts From Kids.* Beltsville, MD: Gryphon House, Inc.

Neugebauer, B. & R. Neugebauer (editors). 1997. *Does Your Team Work Together?* Redmond, WA: Exchange Press.

Neugebauer, B. & R. Neugebauer. 2001. *Staff Challenges: Articles From Child Care Information Exchange.* Redmond, WA: Exchange Press.

Neugebauer, R. (editor). 1994. *Taking Stock.* Redmond, WA: Child Care Information Exchange.

Newstrom, J.W., & E. Scannell. 1980. *Games Trainers Play.* Whitby, Ontario: McGraw-Hill Trade.

Wheelock College. 2000. *The Power of Mentoring.* Boston, MA: Wheelock College.

Websites

Child Care Business
www.childcarebusiness.com
Monster
www.monster.com
Motivate Teachers
www.motivateteachers.com
National Association for the Education of Young Children
www.naeyc.org
The Creative Curriculum Developmental Continuum Assessment Tool Kit *by Teaching Strategies, Inc*
www.teachingstrategies.com

Challenges Related to Children

Articles

Dorn Zotovich, K. 2001. Helping Children Deal With Loss Through the Journaling Process. <www.griefcounselors.com/art_100.htm> (28 February 2003).

Eisenbud, L. Mar/Apr 2002. Working With Non-Traditional Families. *Child Care Information Exchange*, 144, 16-20.

Gambetti, A. Sept/Oct 2002. How to Keep Children Safe, Yet Allow Some Risks Necessary for Learning. *Child Care Information Exchange*, 147.

Gross, T., & S. Guerwitz Clemens. May 2002. Painting a Tragedy: Young Children Process the Events of September 11. *Young Children*, 57 (3), 44-51.

Your Child and Medications. Reprinted with permission from Fact Sheet Series published by The National Institute on Mental Health, Bethesda, MD. <www.kidneeds.com/diagnostic_categories/articles/med.htm> (3 March, 2003).

Books

Allen, K.E., & L.R. Marotz. 2000. *By the Ages: Behavior & Development of Children Prebirth Through 8*. Independence, KY: Delmar Learning.

Appleton, J., N. McCrea, & C. Patterson. 2001. *Do Carrots Make You See Better?* Beltsville, MD: Gryphon House, Inc.

Bailey, B. 2000. *Conscious Discipline*. Oviedo, FL: Loving Guidance.

Bond, R. 1999. *Just Like a Baby*. New York, NY: Little, Brown, & Co. Juvenile.

Brown, L. 1998. *Dinosaurs Divorce*. New York, NY: Little, Brown, & Co. Juvenile.

Bryant, T., & P. Schiller, 1998. *The Values Book*. Beltsville, MD: Gryphon House, Inc.

Clifton, L. 1998. *Everett Anderson's Goodbye*. New York, NY: Henry Holt & Co.

Curtis, J.L. 1996. *Tell Me Again About the Night I Was Born*. New York, NY: HarperCollins.

Engel, J. & I. Prince. 1998. *The Complete Allergy Book*. Westport, CT: Firefly Books.

Fox, M. 1989. *Wilfred Gordon McDonald Partridge*. Glenview, IL: Scott Foresman (Pearson K-12).

Fox, M. 1997. *Sophie*. New York, NY: Voyager Books.

Freedman, M., & E. Weiner. 1999. *Taking Food Allergies to School*. Valley Park, MO: JayJo Books.

Gray, L.M. 1995. *My Mama Had a Dancing Heart*. London, England: Orchard Books.

Green, C.R., PhD. 1999. *Total Memory Workout*. New York, NY: Random House.

Ireton, H., C. Mardell-Czudnowski, & G. Mindes. 1995. *Assessing Young Children*. Independence, KY: Delmar Learning.

Kurland, M., & R.A. Lupoff. 1999. *The Complete Idiot's Guide to Improving Your Memory*. New York, NY: Alpha Books.

Lansky, V. 1999. *Taming of the C.A.N.D.Y. Monster, Continuously Advertised Nutritionally Deficient Yummies: A Cookbook*. Minnetonka, MN: Book Peddlers.

Lee Curtis, J. 1993. *When I Was Little: A Four-Year-Old's Memoir of Her Youth*. New York, NY: HarperCollins Juvenile Books.

McCutcheon, J. 2001. *Happy Adoption Day.* New York, NY: Little, Brown, & Co. Juvenile.

Miller, J. 1991. *The Perfectly Safe Home.* Hartville, OH: William Gray Publishing.

Mundy, M. 1998. *Sad Isn't Bad.* Newry, North Ireland: Abbey Press.

Robertson, C. 2001. *Safety, Nutrition, and Health in Child Care.* Independence, KY: Delmar Learning.

Rogers, F. 1996. *Let's Talk About It: Divorce.* New York, NY: Philomel Books.

Rogers, F. 1996. *The New Baby.* East Rutherford, NJ: Penguin Putnam Books for Young Readers.

Smith, C. 1993. *The Peaceful Classroom.* Beltsville, MD: Gryphon House, Inc.

Smith, N. 2002. *Allie the Allergic Elephant: A Children's Story of Peanut Allergies.* San Francisco, CA: Jungle Communications, Inc.

Tazewell, C. 2001. *The Littlest Angel.* Nashville, TN: Ideals Children's Books.

Whelan, M.S. 2001. *But They Spit, Scratch, and Swear!: The Dos and Don'ts of Behavior Guidance With School-Age Children.* Saint Paul, MN: Redleaf Press.

Wild, M. 1994. *The Very Best of Friends.* New York, NY: Voyager Books.

Websites

Turn the Page Press, Inc.
www.turnthepage.com
American School Food Service Association
www.asfsa.org
SafeKids
www.safekids.com
Perfectly Safe
www.perfectlysafe.com.
National Resource Center for Health and Safety in Child Care
http://nrc.uchsc.edu/index.html#TOP.
Child Health Online
www.childhealthonline.org/parents.htm
healthykids
www.healthykids.com.
Pediatric Guide for Brooklyn Parents
www.spindlepub.com/kids/library/allergy.htm
Allergies
www.cchs.net/health/getcontents.asp?DOCID=center&cID=1
American Disabilities Act
www.usdoj.gov/crt/ada/adahom1.htm
National Information Center for Children and Youth with Disabilities
www.nichcy.org
learnthat
www.learnthat.com/courses/lifestyle/names

Challenges Related to Parents

Articles

ABC's and 123's. Excerpted From the Parent's Guide to Early Childhood Programs by Teaching Strategies. <www.teachingstrategies.com> (3 March, 2003).

Bro, S. 2001. How to Deal with Difficult Parents. *Child Care Business*, 2 (4), 10-18.

Crites-Price, S., & T. Price. Keeping Your Caregiver Happy. <familyfun.go.com/raisingkids/child/skills/feature/dony87prcaregiver/> (3 March, 2003).

DeSteno, N. Nov 2002. Parent Involvement in the Classroom: The Fine Line. *Young Children*, 55 (3), 13-17.

Garcia, V. Summer 1999. Understanding and Preventing Toddler Biting. *Texas Child Care Quarterly*, 23(1), 12.

Golden, A. Working With Your Child's Caregiver. *Ohio State University Extension Fact Sheet.* <http://ohioline.osu.edu/hyg-fact/5000/5205.html> (28 February, 2003).

Greenman, J. March/April 2001. Empowering Parents? *Child Care Information Exchange*, 138, p. 56-59.

Harris, J. Sept/Oct 1994. The Bad News Blues: When Messages Aren't Easy to Deliver. *Child Care Information Exchange*, 99, 36-38.

Hilliard, D. Sept/Oct 2002. Making Families Welcome. *Child Care Information Exchange*, 147, 45-46.

Kieff, J., & K. Welhousen. May 2000. Planning Family Involvement in Early Childhood Programs. *Young Children*, 55 (3), 18-25.

New, R.S. Mar 1999. Here, We Call It "Drop Off and Pick Up": Transition to Child Care, American-Style. *Young Children*, 54 (2), 34-35.

Paxton, R. 2002. Saving Family Keepsakes for Scrapbooking. <www.creativehomemaking.com/articles/092402a.shtml> (3 March, 2003).

Pelo, A. Sept/Oct 2002. From Borders to Bridges: Transforming Our Relationships with Parents. *Child Care Information Exchange*, 147, 38-41.

Redleaf National Institute. How to Create Contacts and Policies. From Getting Started in the Business of Family Child Care. <www.redleafinstitute.org/Index.cfm?section=BL&Page=BL10> (3 March, 2003).

Schwinn, E. Charlotte Parent: Saving Vacation Memories. <www.familyfun.go.com/crafts/cutpaste/feature/char38scraps/char38scraps.html> (3 March, 2003).

Books

Britz, J., P. Jorde Bloom, & M. Sheerer. 1991. *Blueprint for Action: Achieving Center Based Change Through Staff Development.* Lake Forest, Il: New Horizon.

Charnov, D., & C. Rutsch. 2000. *Making a Difference: A Parent's Guide to Advocacy and Community Action.* Washington, DC: Children's Resources International.

Elkind, D. 2001. *The Hurried Child.* Cambridge, MA: Perseus Publishing.

Greenman, J. 1998. *Places for Childhoods: Making Quality Happen in the Real World.*
    Redmond, WA: Child Care Information Exchange.

Guthrie, E., & K. Matthews. 2002. *The Trouble With Perfect: How Parents Avoid the Over
    Achievement Trap and Still Raise Successful Children.* New York, NY: Broadway Books.

Murphy Yates, S. 2002. *The Busy Mom.* Washington, DC: Child Welfare League of America.

Trister Dodge, D. 1998. *Preschool for Parents: What Every Parent Needs to Know About
    Preschool.* Naperville, IL: Sourcebooks Trade.

Websites

Tips for Choosing Child Care

www.childcaredirectory.com/tips.html

The Child Care Group

www.childcaregroup.org

Life Advice About Your Child's First Day at School

www.pueblo.gsa.gov/cic_text/children/firstday/firstday.htm

Activities

www.npin.org/library/2001/n00564/2.html

The Parent Club

www.theparentclub.com

Family Education Network

www.familyeducation.com

ChildCareExchange.com

www.childcareexchange.com

Teaching Strategies, Inc.

www.teachingstrategies.com

The National Association for the Education of Young Children

www.naeyc.org

Family Communications

misterrogers.org/early_care/using_mrn_fc_pamphlets.asp

Family Internet

www.familyinternet.about.com/library/weekly

Challenges Related to the Details of Directing a Center

Articles

Bess, G., & C. Ratekin. Nov/Dec 2000. Orienting and Evaluating Your Board of Directors. *Child Care Information Exchange*, 136, 82-87.

Gellens, S. Sept/Oct 1994. Paralyzed by Personal Stress: A Director's Story. *Child Care Information Exchange*, 99, 11-14.

Miles, K. Aug/Sept 2000. Internet as a Relevant Marketing Tool. *Child Care Business*, 1(1) 36.

Mitcham, K. Mar 2001. Identifying What You Need in a Jungle of Paper Work. *Child Care Business*, 2(3), 10.

Morgan, H.M. Jan 2001. A Director's Lot Is Not a Happy Lot. *Child Care Information Exchange*, 137, 8-10.

Talley, K. L. Sept/Oct 1997. How Are You Doing? A Center Director Self-Review Tool. *Child Care Information Exchange*, 117, 17-23.

Targos, R. Nov 2000. Welcome to the World of the Web. *Child Care Business*, 1(3), 40.

Wassom, J. Jul/Aug, 2000. Power Pack Your Center Brochure. *Child Care Information Exchange*. 134, 16-17.

Wassom, J. May/Jun 2002. The Way of the Web. *Child Care Information Exchange*. 145, 11-14.

Books

Baldwin, S., & M.S. Whelan (editors). 1996. *Lifesavers: Tips for Success and Sanity for Early Childhood Managers*. Stillwater, MN: Insights, Training, and Consulting.

Baldwin, S., & R.A. Wray. 1999. *Lighten Up and Live Longer: A Collection of Jokes, Anecdotes, and Stories Guaranteed to Tickle Your Soul*. Stillwater, MN: Insights, Training, and Consulting.

Carter, M., & D. Curtis. 1998. *The Visionary Director*. Saint Paul, MN: Redleaf Press.

Dichtelmiller, M., A.L. Dombro, & J. Jablon. 1999. *The Power of Observation*. Washington, DC: Teaching Strategies.

Foster-Jorgenson, K., & A. Harrington. *Financial Management for the Childcare Executive Officer*. Saint Paul, MN: Redleaf Press.

Leeds, D. 1987. *Smart Questions: A New Strategy for Successful Managers*. New York, NY: McGraw-Hill.

Leonard, A.M. 1997. *I Spy Something: A Practical Guide for Using Observation Tools in the Preschool Classroom*. Little Rock, AK: Southern Association on Children Under Six.

Morgan, G. 1999. *The Bottom Line for Children's Programs*. Watertown, MA: Steam Press.

Neugebauer, R. (editor). 1994. *Taking Stock*. Redmond, WA: Child Care Information Exchange Press.

Powers, E.A.N. *The Boring Book of Forms, Volume I: Every Employee Form You Will Ever Need* (upcoming title).

Videos

Observing Young Children by Teaching Strategies. Contact www.teachingstrategies.com.

Websites

Child Care Networking
www.geocities.com/Athens/Forum/5274/loops.html
Kolbe Corp.
www.kolbe.com
STARS for Early Care and Education
www.earlychildhoodresources.com
ART Enterprises
www.artenterprises.com.
Georgia Association on Young Children
www.gayconline.org
Day-Timer
www.daytimer.com
Turn the Page Press, Inc.
www.turnthepage.com
homefurnish.com
www.homefurnish.com/deco3.htm#cozy

Challenges Related to the Center

Articles

Basile, C., & C. White. Summer 2000. Environmental Education: A Walk in the Park Is Just the Beginning. *Dimensions of Early Childhood*, 28 (3), 3-7.

Carter, M., & A. Pelo. July/Aug 2002. Moving Staff Through Difficult Issues. *Child Care Information Exchange*, 146, p. 25.

Eisenberg, E. Sept/Oct 1997. Meeting Adult Needs Within the Classroom. *Child Care Information Exchange*, 117, 53-56.

Ginsberg, S.I., & L.C. Whitehead. 1999. Creating a Family-Like Atmosphere in Child Care Settings: All the More Difficult in Large Child Care Centers. *Young Children*, 54 (2), 4-10.

Kieschnich, M.M. Building a Healthy Preschool Director-Pastor Relationship. <www.elca.org/lp/preschl.html> (3 March, 2003).

Targos, R. Jun/Jul 2001. Lock Up: Securing Your Building. *Child Care Business*, 2 (6), 32-35.

Young Children (May 2002) 57(3), 8-42. Several articles on outdoor play.

Books

Appleton, J., N. McCrea, & C. Patterson. 2001. *Do Carrots Make You See Better?* Beltsville, MD: Gryphon House, Inc.

Exelby, B., & R. Isbell. 2001. *Early Learning Environments That Work*. Beltsville, MD: Gryphon House, Inc.

Greenman, J. 1998. *Places for Childhoods: Making Quality Happen in the Real World.*

Redmond, WA: Child Care Information Exchange.

Lombardi, J. 2002. *Time to Care: Redesigning Child Care to Promote Education, Support Families, and build Communities.* Philadelphia, PA: Temple University Press.

Rockwell, R.E., E.A. Sherwood, & R.A. Williams. 1990. *Hug a Tree.* Beltsville, MD: Gryphon House, Inc.

Rybolt, T.R., & L.M. Rybolt. 2002. *Science Fair Success With Scents, Aromas, and Smells.* Berkeley Heights, NJ: Enslow Publishers, Inc.

Websites

FASTSIGNS
www.fastsigns.com/products/banner
The Better Business Bureau
www.betterbusinessbureau.org.
The Bread Beckers, Inc.
www.breadbeckers.com
Child Care Business
www.childcarebusiness.com
Georgia Emergency Management Agency
http://www.gema.state.ga.us/

Challenges Related to the Community

Articles

Pendleton, K. Are We There Yet? Take a Chance and Plan a Field Trip. <http://www.canr.uconn.edu/ces/child/newsarticles/FCC842.html> (28 February, 2003).

Wassom, J. May/Jun 2001. Community Marketing Made Easy. *Child Care Information Exchange*, 139, 18-20.

Weiss, T. Starting a Support Group. <http://www.parentsinc.org/newsletter/2001/supportgroup.html> (28 February, 2003).

Alvarado, C. (facilitator). Jan/Feb 2002. Voices in Search of Cultural Continuity in Communities. *Child Care Information Exchange*, 143, 42-44.

Websites

Habitat for Humanity
www.habitat.org
The National Association for the Education of Young Children
www.naeyc.org

Index